# LIFE
## CENTERED
### CAREER
### EDUCATION
ACTIVITY

BOOK

TWO

**Lynda Gayle
Glascoe
and
Lynn Sharon
Miller
with
Charles J.
Kokaska**

A product of the ERIC Clearinghouse on Handicapped and Gifted Children
The Council for Exceptional Children

**Library of Congress Cataloging-in-Publication Data**

Glascoe, Lynda Gayle.
  Life centered career education.

  "A product of the ERIC Clearinghouse on Handicapped and
Gifted Children."
  Includes index.
    1. Career education—United States—Curricula.
2. Activity programs in education—United States.
3. Exceptional children—Education—United States—Curricula.  I. Miller,
Lynn Sharon.  II. Kokaska, Charles J.  III. Council for Exceptional Chil-
dren.  IV. ERIC Clearinghouse on Handicapped and Gifted Chil-
dren.  V. Title.
LC1037.5.G52  1986          371.9          85-28069
ISBN 0-86586-163-3 (pbk. : v. 2)

Published in 1986 by The Council for Exceptional Children,
1920 Association Drive, Reston, Virginia 22091-1589
Stock No. 304          Price $9.95

*Office of Educational
Research and Improvement*

This publication was prepared with funding from the U.S. Department of
Education, Office of Educational Research and Improvement, contract no. 400-
84-0010. Contractors undertaking such projects under government sponsorship
are encouraged to express freely their judgment in professional and technical
matters. Prior to publication the manuscript was submitted to The Council for
Exceptional Children for critical review and determination of professional
competence. This publication has met such standards. Points of view, however,
do not necessarily represent the official view or opinions of either The Council
for Exceptional Children or the Department of Education.

# Contents

Acknowledgments ................................................................ iv

About the Authors .............................................................. iv

Introduction ....................................................................... 1

1. Daily Living Skills Activities ........................................ 5

2. Personal-Social Skills Activities ................................. 40

3. Occupational Skills Activities ..................................... 70

Index .................................................................................. 99

# Acknowledgments

The authors thank the following people who were instrumental in the development of this text.

*Donn E. Brolin* for encouraging us to expand on his ideas; *Paul J. Perencevic* for reviewing our first efforts; *Penny Sue Peters* and *Christine Hughes* for their practical advice and inspiration; *Wayne* and *Doris Henthorn* for providing us with a peaceful place to work; *Jean Nazzaro* and *June Jordan* for a chance to publish; and *our families*, Greg, Scott, Derek, Sharen, and Laurel, for their support and patience.

# About the Authors

Lynda Gayle Glascoe, M.S., Special Education, teaches in a junior high Resource Specialist Program, Garden Grove Unified School District, Garden Grove, California.

Lynn Sharon Miller, M.S., Special Education, teaches an elementary Special Day Class for the Severely Handicapped, Garden Grove Unified School District, Garden Grove, California.

Charles J. Kokaska, Ed.D., teaches at California State University, Long Beach and co-authored with Donn E. Brolin the textbook *Career Education for Handicapped Individuals, 2nd edition.*

# Introduction

This book and its companion, *Life Centered Career Education: Activity Book One*, are direct descendants of another successful publication of The Council for Exceptional Children, *Life Centered Career Education: A Competency Based Approach* (Brolin, 1978, 1983). These two new activity books add to the Life Centered curriculum by providing planned activities to be used with elementary and secondary school students. The concept behind the Life Centered Career Education approach is to infuse life skills into the basic curriculum. The material provided in Activity Books One and Two give students practice with academic skills in practical contexts. Although Book Two is specifically designed for the adolescent or older student, many of the activities in Book One may need to be practiced by these students as well. It is suggested that teachers refer to both books before selecting the activity that best meets the needs of their unique group of students.

The Life Centered Career Education curriculum organizes 22 major competencies and 102 subcompetencies into three domains: Daily Living Skills, Personal-Social Skills, and Occupational Skills. A complete overview of the competencies appears in Figure 1.

The Life Centered Career Education competencies were originally designed for instruction with mildly mentally retarded secondary students. This approach, however, has been used in regular classrooms and with other types of exceptional learners at both elementary and middle school levels.

## Organization

Each book is divided into the three major domains: Daily Living Skills, Personal-Social Skills, and Occupational Skills. Within each domain the activities are identified by their corresponding competency and subcompetency. Those who have used the original Brolin material will find this format familiar. Activities are presented so that the type of activity, the academic components, resource persons, and follow-up/evaluation are listed in the margin. To use selectively, teachers would refer to Figure 1 to identify the subcompetency and then turn to the corresponding lesson in Book One or Two. An index is provided that lists activities by type—e.g., role play—and by academic component—e.g., math.

## Considerations

Activities are designed to use materials and supplies normally available to most teachers. Teacher-made props, games, forms, and worksheets are described and samples are provided where appropriate. No special purchases of curriculum materials are required for these activities.

In many cases, teachers may have developed lesson plans similar to those presented. The activities in these books provide only one suggestion at each level for the subcompetencies. These suggestions are not intended to displace but rather to augment the teacher's own ideas. These books will be especially valuable if the Life Centered Career Education curriculum is already installed in a school. Two of the authors are special education teachers who have tested these materials in their elementary and middle school classrooms with a range of handicapped students. As you use these activities and become involved in creating or improvising your own, you are urged to submit your activities for additional volumes of this series. Send your ideas to Life Centered Career Education Activities, Department of Information Services, The Council for Exceptional Children, 1920 Association Drive, Reston, VA 22091-1589.

## Reference

Brolin, D. (1978, revised 1983). *Life Centered Career Education: A Competency Based Approach*. Reston, VA: The Council for Exceptional Children.

| Curriculum Area | Competency | Subcompetencies | |
|---|---|---|---|
| **Daily Living Skills** | 1. Managing Family Finances | 1. Identify money and make correct change | 2. Make wise expenditures |
| | 2. Selecting, Managing, and Maintaining a Home | 6. Select adequate housing | 7. Maintain a home |
| | 3. Caring for Personal Needs | 10. Dress appropriately | 11. Exhibit proper grooming and hygiene |
| | 4. Raising Children, Enriching Family Living | 14. Prepare for adjustment to marriage | 15. Prepare for raising children (physical care) |
| | 5. Buying and Preparing Food | 18. Demonstrate appropriate eating skills | 19. Plan balanced meals |
| | 6. Buying and Caring for Clothing | 24. Wash clothing | 25. Iron and store clothing |
| | 7. Engaging in Civic Activities | 28. Generally understand local laws & government | 29. Generally understand Federal Government |
| | 8. Utilizing Recreation and Leisure | 34. Participate actively in group activities | 35. Know activities and available community resources |
| | 9. Getting around the Community (Mobility) | 40. Demonstrate knowledge of traffic rules & safety practices | 41. Demonstrate knowledge & use of various means of transportation |
| **Personal-Social Skills** | 10. Achieving Self Awareness | 43. Attain a sense of body | 44. Identify interests and abilities |
| | 11. Acquiring Self Confidence | 48. Express feelings of worth | 49. Tell how others see him/her |
| | 12. Achieving Socially Responsible Behavior | 53. Know character traits needed for acceptance | 54. Know proper behavior in public places |
| | 13. Maintaining Good Interpersonal Skills | 58. Know how to listen and respond | 59. Know how to make & maintain friendships |
| | 14. Achieving Independence | 62. Understand impact of behaviors upon others | 63. Understand self organization |
| | 15. Achieving Problem Solving Skills | 66. Differentiate bipolar concepts | 67. Understand the need for goals |
| | 16. Communicating Adequately with Others | 71. Recognize emergency situations | 72. Read at level needed for future goals |
| **Occupational Guidance & Preparation** | 17. Knowing & Exploring Occupational Possibilities | 76. Identify the personal values met through work | 77. Identify the societal values met through work |
| | 18. Selecting & Planning Occupational Choices | 82. Identify major occupational needs | 83. Identify major occupational interests |
| | 19. Exhibiting Appropriate Work Habits & Behaviors | 87. Follow directions | 88. Work with others |
| | 20. Exhibiting Sufficient Physical-Manual Skills | 94. Demonstrate satisfactory balance and coordination | 95. Demonstrate satisfactory manual dexterity |
| | 21. Obtaining a Specific Occupational Skill | | |
| | 22. Seeking, Securing, & Maintaining Employment | 98. Search for a job | 99. Apply for a job |

# FIGURE 1
## Life Centered Career Education Competencies

| | | | | |
|---|---|---|---|---|
| 3. Obtain and use bank and credit facilities | 4. Keep basic financial records | 5. Calculate and pay taxes | | |
| 8. Use basic appliances and tools | 9. Maintain home exterior | | | |
| 12. Demonstrate knowledge of physical fitness, nutrition, & weight control | 13. Demonstrate knowledge of common illness prevention and treatment | | | |
| 16. Prepare for raising children (psychological care) | 17. Practice family safety in the home | | | |
| 20. Purchase food | 21. Prepare meals | 22. Clean food preparation areas | 23. Store food | |
| 26. Perform simple mending | 27. Purchase clothing | | | |
| 30. Understand citizenship rights and responsibilities | 31. Understand registration and voting procedures | 32. Understand Selective Service procedures | 33. Understand civil rights & responsibilities when questioned by the law | |
| 36. Understand recreational values | 37. Use recreational facilities in the community | 38. Plan and choose activities wisely | 39. Plan vacations | |
| 42. Drive a car | | | | |
| 45. Identify emotions | 46. Identify needs | 47. Understand the physical self | | |
| 50. Accept praise | 51. Accept criticism | 52. Develop confidence in self | | |
| 55. Develop respect for the rights and properties of others | 56. Recognize authority and follow instructions | 57. Recognize personal roles | | |
| 60. Establish appropriate heterosexual relationships | 61. Know how to establish close relationships | | | |
| 64. Develop goal seeking behavior | 65. Strive toward self actualization | | | |
| 68. Look at alternatives | 69. Anticipate consequences | 70. Know where to find good advice | | |
| 73. Write at the level needed for future goals | 74. Speak adequately for understanding | 75. Understand the subtleties of communication | | |
| 78. Identify the remunerative aspects of work | 79. Understand classification of jobs into different occupational systems | 80. Identify occupational opportunities available locally | 81. Identify sources of occupational information | |
| 84. Identify occupational aptitudes | 85. Identify requirements of appropriate and available jobs | 86. Make realistic occupational choices. | | |
| 89. Work at a satisfactory rate | 90. Accept supervision | 91. Recognize the importance of attendance and punctuality | 92. Meet demands for quality work | 93. Demonstrate occupational safety |
| 96. Demonstrate satisfactory stamina and endurance | 97. Demonstrate satisfactory sensory discrimination | | | |
| | | | | |
| 100. Interview for a job | 101. Adjust to competitive standards | 102. Maintain postschool occupational adjustment | | |

# 1. Daily Living Skills

## Competencies

1. Managing Family Finances
2. Selecting, Managing, and Maintaining a Home
3. Caring for Personal Needs
4. Raising Children, Enriching Family Living
5. Buying and Preparing Food
6. Buying and Caring for Clothing
7. Engaging in Civic Activities
8. Utilizing Recreation and Leisure
9. Getting around the Community (Mobility)

**Domain:** Daily Living Skills
**Competency:** 1. Managing Family Finances
**Subcompetency:** 1. Identifying Money and Making Correct Change

## Count Your Change

*Academic Component*

   Math

*Type of Activity*

   Role Play

*Objective*

   When making a purchase, the student will be able to determine whether or not the change received is correct.

*Activity*

   This role-playing activity involves two or more students. One student is the "cus-tomer," the other is the "clerk" or "cash-ier." Real or play money (coins and bills) is used.

1. Situations are presented to the stu-dents on 3″ × 5″ cards.

   Example: Customer buys three pencils at 19¢ each. He gives the clerk a $1 bill.

   Example: Customer buys a pair of shoes for $22.43. He gives the clerk a $20 bill and a $10 bill.

2. The customer gives the clerk the amount of money indicated on the card.
3. The clerk gives the change to the customer.
4. The customer counts the change to determine whether or not it is correct. (The teacher can instruct the clerk to occasionally give the incorrect change.)
5. A calculator can be used to check accuracy.

6. Note: The customer should identify the change as incorrect even if he is given more than he should have.

*Follow-up; Evaluation*

Given an amount of purchase, money paid, and change received, the student correctly identifies the change as correct or incorrect.

---

**Domain:** Daily Living Skills
**Competency:** 1. Managing Family Finances
**Subcompetency:** 2. Making Wise Expenditures

---

# Spend Your Money Wisely

*Academic Components*

Math
Reading

*Type of Activity*

Research

*Objective*

Given a specific budget, the student will be able to purchase an item or items at the best price possible.

*Activity*

Bring to class several newspaper ads, catalogs, and/or sales flyers from a variety of stores.
1. Discuss making wise expenditures, including the purchase of clothing, food, appliances, furniture, luxury items, etc. Discuss the use of discount stores, sales, and store brands as a way to save money.
2. Give each student a 3″ × 5″ card with a different assignment. Be sure the items assigned can be located in the available ads and catalogs. Provide a space for the student to record the price of the item(s) and the name of the store. (See examples.)

*Example*: You have $20.00
You need to buy a pair of jogging shoes.
Jogging shoes cost:
$_____ at _____(name of store)
$_____ at _____
$_____ at _____
Best price: _____

*Example*: You have $1.00.
You need to buy toothpaste.
Toothpaste costs:
$_____ at _____
$_____ at _____
$_____ at _____
Best price: _____

3. Students look at various ads and/or catalogs to locate the best purchase prices. (The teacher and aide may have to assist students in this activity. For students with low reading skills, locate the items for them and have them compare the prices.)
4. Discuss differences in quality among products. The cheapest product may not be the best buy if it does not meet the needs of the buyer.

*Follow-up; Evaluation*

The student compares the prices of two or more similar items and chooses the one at the best price.

*Related Activities*

These and similar activities can be used to form a banking unit to be continued throughout the school year. (See "Opening a Checking Account" and "Using a Checkbook.")

**Domain:** Daily Living Skills
**Competency:** 1. Managing Family Finances
**Subcompetency:** 3. Obtaining and Using Bank and Credit Facilities

# Opening a Checking Account

*Academic Components*

Reading
Language (Vocabulary)
Language (Written
    Expression)

*Type of Activity*

Role Play

*Objectives*

1. The student will be able to correctly complete an application for a bank account.
2. The student will demonstrate proper behavior in a bank.

*Activity*

Obtain account application cards from a bank or make your own (see example). Use the actual terminology found on application cards. A large facsimile of the card may be drawn on the chalkboard or poster paper.

1. Discuss terms used in the application.
2. Fill out large facsimile, discussing each step.
3. Give each student an application to complete.
4. Stress neatness and correct spelling.
5. The teacher and/or aide acts as the bank teller. The students wait in line as applications are completed.
6. The teacher checks accuracy and neatness of application card. The teller gives the student a checkbook (to be used in future classroom banking activities) and welcomes the customer to __(School)__ National Bank. (Call the students "Miss ____" and "Mr. ____" when doing banking activities.)

*Follow-up; Evaluation*

1. Application is completed correctly and neatly.
2. Proper behavior for a bank is maintained:
   (a) The student waits patiently in line.
   (b) The student talks in a normal tone of voice.
   (c) The student is polite to other customers and bank employees.

## Checking Account Application Card

Checking Account      Acct. No. _____
                                        (For Bank Use Only)

Please open a __(School name)__ Checking Account as follows:
Account is to be set up in the following name(s) _____
_____

Signature _____
Signature _____
Address _____
         Street and No.        City         State        Zip
Employed by _____
          Firm Name                 Position
Social Security Number _____ Date _____
Opening Deposit: Check # _____ Amount _____

This account is accepted by __(School)__ National Bank and subject to the provisions stated on the reverse side of this card. Above are the duly authorized signatures which the Bank will recognize in the payment of funds or the transaction of other business.

**Domain:** Daily Living Skills
**Competency:** 1. Managing Family Finances
**Subcompetency:** 4. Keeping Basic Financial Records

# Using a Checkbook

*Academic Components*

Math
Language (Written
Expression)

*Types of Activity*

Discussion
Role Play

*Objectives*

1. The student will be able to correctly endorse and deposit a check.
2. The student will record deposits and checks written in a register and maintain an accurate balance.
3. The student will demonstrate appropriate behavior in a bank.

*Activities*

After a checking account has been opened by the student (see "Opening a Checking Account"), the following basic plan is used for each lesson in a banking unit. See example.

Note: Use role playing whenever possible.

*1. Paycheck*

Pay can be based on points earned for proper behavior or completed classwork. Each paycheck should be $100 to $300 for each activity.

The amount of each student's paycheck will vary. Discuss this with the class. Students who are frequently tardy, or do not always complete class work, will earn fewer points and will consequently have smaller paychecks than others. Students who consistently follow directions will earn more. Discuss implications for "real-life" situations.

Discuss parts of the check and demonstrate proper endorsement of the check.

*2. Deposit*

Obtain deposit slips from a bank or commercial banking unit, or make your own. Draw a large facsimile of the deposit slip on the chalkboard or poster paper to demonstrate proper completion.

Students fill out deposit slip, using information on their paychecks. Role play depositing a check at the bank.

*3. Maintaining a Register*

Each student is given a checkbook at the time of application. Obtain commercial checkbook registers, or make your own. The two-line entry format is best to use for the students.

Use a large facsimile to demonstrate making entries and adding or subtracting to maintain an accurate balance.

Allow the students to use calculators.

Every time a banking activity is done, review when to add and when to subtract, and the importance of keeping the balance accurate and up to date.

**Deposit Slip**

| Date _____ | Coin | | |
| Account no. _____ | Currency | | |
| Name _____ | Checks: | | |
| Address _____ | | | |
| _____ | | | |
| Phone _____ | Total | | |

**Check Register**

| Date | Check # | Transaction | Balance forward | | |
|------|---------|-------------|-----------------|---|---|
| ...... | ...... | ...................... | ...................... | | ...... |
| ...... | ...... | ...................... | ...................... | | ...... |
| ...... | ...... | ...................... | ...................... | | ...... |

*4. Writing Checks*

Provide a variety of activities for making purchases. The students follow directions for each lesson and write checks as indicated. Again, demonstrate on board or with a poster.

It is helpful to have a chart available to the students on the spelling of number words. Practice writing dollars and cents correctly.

*Follow-up; Evaluation*

1. As the student makes deposit, check for accuracy of endorsement and completion of deposit slip.
2. After each lesson, check each student's check register for accuracy of completion, addition, and subtraction.

**Check**

| | |
|---|---|
| Name _____ | Check Number _____ |
| Address _____ | Date _____ |
| Phone _____ | |
| Pay to the order of _____ $_____ |
| _____ Dollars |
| Memo _____    _____ |

*Related Activities*

"Spend Your Money Wisely"
"Opening a Checking Account"
"Grocery Shopping"
"Planning and Buying a School Wardrobe"

**Domain:** Daily Living Skills
**Competency:** 1. Managing Family Finances
**Subcompetency:** 5. Calculating and Paying Taxes

# How Much Sales Tax?

*Academic Component*

Math

*Types of Activity*

Discussion
Demonstration

*Objective*

The student will be able to calculate sales tax on a variety of purchases using multiplication and/or a tax chart.

*Activity*

1. Conduct a class discussion on sales taxes. Include the following information:
   (a) Reasons for sales tax
   (b) Tax rate in your state; local sales tax, if any
   (c) Uses of sales tax in your state
   (d) Types of items taxed
2. Bring to class sales receipts for various items: groceries, clothing, gasoline, home furnishings, etc. The students examine receipts to locate sales tax and note which items are taxed and which items are not taxed.
3. Demonstrate the use of multiplication to determine sales tax.
   (a) Do several examples on the board. Demonstrate the use of a calculator to determine sales tax.
   (b) Provide students with ads from newspapers. Each student chooses at least five items, and calculates tax on each purchase price. Students may use calculators.
4. Repeat exercise 3, using a tax chart.

*Follow-up; Evaluation*

1. Given the sales price of three items, the student correctly calculates sales tax, using multiplication, calculator, or tax chart.

**Domain:** Daily Living Skills
**Competency:** 2. Selecting, Managing, and Maintaining a Home
**Subcompetency:** 6. Selecting Adequate Housing

# Renting an Apartment

*Academic Components*

Reading
Language (Oral Expression)

*Type of Activity*

Role Play

*Objectives*

1. The student will demonstrate skill in using newspaper classified ads to search for housing within a specific budget.
2. The student will be able to make a telephone call to inquire about adequate housing.
3. The student will be able to complete a rental application form.
4. The student will demonstrate appropriate conduct in an interview with a landlord.

*Activity One*

Have several copies of local newspaper classified ads available.
1. Using a chalkboard, poster, or overhead projector, show the students how and where to locate categories for housing in the classified ads (Furnished and Unfurnished Houses and Apartments, Houses for Sale, Rooms for Rent, etc.).
2. Each student locates given catagories in a copy of the newspaper. Repeat the search as often as needed.
3. Print a monthly housing budget and general geographic location on a 3" × 5" card for each student. Example: $450–$475, Garden Grove.
4. The student finds and circles two or three ads which meet the qualifications on the card. The student should copy information on another piece of paper including phone number of the renter.
Note: Adaptations for students who are unable to copy the information:
   (a) The student circles the appropriate ad in red ink.
   (b) The student cuts or tears out the appropriate ad.
   (c) Another student copies the ad.

*Follow-up; Evaluation*

The student correctly locates and copies information about rental property from the classified section of the newspaper.

*Activity Two*

This is a role-playing activity using information obtained from the newspaper in the previous activity. If possible, have two telephones in the classroom.
1. With the class, make a list of further information needed about the rental properties in the chosen ads (deposit, pets, utilities, etc.).
2. The student "calls" the number given in the newspaper ad to request more information. The teacher, aide, or another student can be on the other telephone.
3. Using appropriate rules of telephone courtesy, the student asks questions and jots down the answers as given.
4. The student ends the call in a polite manner.
5. The student repeats the call for other ads.

*Follow-up; Evaluation*

1. The student is polite and asks appropriate questions when inquiring about a rental property.
2. Using the information obtained from the newspaper and telephone call, the student determines whether or not each facility meets his or her requirements (according to the card presented to the student in the first activity).

*Activity Three*

1. The student selects one or more available rental units to "visit."
2. The teacher, aide, or another student acts as the "landlord."
3. After setting up an appointment on the telephone, the student visits the landlord to view the property and ask more questions or reinforce information obtained by telephone.
4. The landlord gives the student a rental application to be filled out. Discuss terms and information requested on the rental application form. The student completes the application. (Rental applications can be obtained at most office supply stores.)

*Follow-up; Evaluation*

1. The student is polite while visiting a prospective landlord.
2. The student completes a rental application correctly and neatly.

**Domain:** Daily Living Skills
**Competency:** 2. Selecting, Managing, and Maintaining a Home
**Subcompetency:** 7. Maintaining a Home
                       9. Maintaining a Home Exterior

# Self-Evaluation: Home Maintenance

*Academic Component*

Language (Oral Expression)

*Types of Activity*

Discussion
Worksheet

*School/Community Resource Persons*

Home-maintenance personnel

*Objective*

Given a skill needed in maintaining a home or home exterior, the student will evaluate personal skill and interest in performing that task.

*Activity*

Most of the skills in maintaining a home's interior and exterior are best taught in the home, industrial arts classes, and home economics classes. However, discussions can be held in the Resource or Special Education classroom.
1. Discuss some of the skills that are needed in maintaining a home: cleaning, simple repairs, painting, and gardening.
2. Discuss jobs that are usually performed by the individual and those that are usually performed by a professional.
3. Discuss the pros and cons of hiring a professional to do jobs such as:
   (a) painting
   (b) gardening
   (c) plumbing
   (d) electrical wiring
   (e) housecleaning
   (f) carpet and furniture cleaning
   (g) roof repair
   (h) window washing
   (i) furniture moving
   (j) window or screen replacement
   (k) appliance repair
4. Give students a checklist of several skills. (Students can help prepare this list.) Students evaluate personal skill and interest in performing the skills (see worksheet).

*Follow-up; Evaluation*

The student completes "Home Skills— Self-Evaluation" worksheet, evaluating interest and ability in performing home maintenance skills.

*Related Activity*

Professionals who perform home maintenance skills may be invited to the classroom to discuss the services they perform for homeowners. (Suggestions: plumber, painter, housekeeper, gardener, appliance repairman, electrician)

**Worksheet**
*Home Skills — Self-Evaluation*

| Directions: For each skill, answer "Yes" or "No" to all four questions. | | | | |
|---|---|---|---|---|
| *Skill* | *Can you do this now?* | *Do you think you will do it when older?* | *Do you enjoy doing it?* | *Would it be a good idea to hire someone to do it?* |
| Dust | | | | |
| Vacuum | | | | |
| Shampoo carpet | | | | |
| Wash windows | | | | |
| Paint inside | | | | |
| Paint outside | | | | |
| Mow lawn | | | | |
| Water lawn | | | | |
| Pull weeds | | | | |
| Trim trees | | | | |
| Fix roof | | | | |
| Repair faucet | | | | |
| Repair wiring | | | | |
| Replace screen | | | | |
| Replace window | | | | |

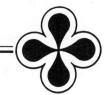

**Domain:** Daily Living Skills
**Competency:** 2. Selecting, Managing, and Maintaining a Home
**Subcompetency:** 8. Using Basic Appliances and Tools

# Reading an Owner's Manual

*Academic Components*

Reading
Language (Vocabulary)
Language (Oral Expression)
Language (Written Expression)

*Types of Activity*

Discussion
Small Group
Demonstration

*Objective*

The student will be able to demonstrate proper use and care of a household appliance by reading the following instructions given in an owner's manual.

*Activity*

Have one or several household appliances available (iron, toaster, vacuum cleaner, etc.) along with the corresponding owner's manual.
1. Discuss difficult vocabulary words that may be found in an owner's manual: *electrical hazard, disconnect, shock, immerse, authorized dealer, defective.*

2. Read the instructions orally (more advanced students may be able to do the reading independently).
3. Students work in small groups or individually to answer questions about the assigned appliance:

   (a) List possible uses for this appliance.
   (b) List some things you should never do with this appliance.
   (c) How should you clean it?
   (d) What should you do if your appliance breaks?
   (e) Is there a warranty? For how long? Any special conditions?
   (f) List any words you do not know.

4. Each group or student reports on an appliance. Discuss words listed in exercise 3f.
5. Students individually demonstrate one aspect of how the appliance should be used or cleaned.

*Follow-up; Evaluation*

The student safely and accurately follows directions when demonstrating the use of a household appliance.

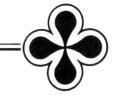

**Domain:** Daily Living Skills
**Competency:** 2. Selecting, Managing, and Maintaining a Home
**Subcompetency:** 9. Maintaining the Home Exterior

# Exterior Maintenance Jobs at School

*Academic Component*

Language (Oral Expression)

*Types of Activity*

Demonstration
Discussion

*School/Community Resource Persons*

Custodial personnel
Grounds maintenance personnel
Parents

*Objective*

The student will adequately perform at least one home exterior maintenance task at school.

*Activity*

The teacher should meet with the principal and a representative of the custodial or grounds maintenance staff before beginning this activity. Identify one or several maintenance tasks the students can become involved in at school. Some examples are: planting and maintaining a garden, or painting a fence or handball court.

1. Invite the custodian to the class to explain the maintenance tasks performed at school that are similar to tasks at home.
2. Describe the exterior maintenance task(s) the students can do at school.
3. Discuss the following questions with the students. Write answers on the board:
   (a) What skills are needed to perform this task? List individual steps taken to complete the job.
   (b) What materials are needed?
   (c) How many people are needed?
   (d) How long should the job take?

4. With the class, develop a schedule for working on this task. Each student should be assigned a part of the task to perform, and a time. Make a chart of the schedule, to be placed on a bulletin board. If it is a long-term project, such as a garden, allow the students to work on different parts of the task at different times.
5. The teacher, custodian, or aide should supervise the students when working on the task.

*Follow-up; Evaluation*

1. At the completion of the project, the person(s) supervising completes an evaluation form for each student participating. (See example.)
2. If this is a long-term project, evaluate periodically.
3. Discuss evaluations with each student. Praise the positive comments. Together, discuss areas to improve.
4. If this is a short-term project, have the students inspect the work several weeks or months later. Does it need to be done again?
5. A similar activity and evaluation can be done at home with parents and/or neighbors.

**Evaluation Form—Exterior Maintenance**

Name of Student:
Name of Supervisor:
Specific Task:
Dates of Task:

Rate the performance of the student in each of the following areas:

|  | *Poor* |  |  |  | *Excellent* |
|---|---|---|---|---|---|
| 1. Promptness to begin work | 1 | 2 | 3 | 4 | 5 |
| 2. Use of time | 1 | 2 | 3 | 4 | 5 |
| 3. Use of materials | 1 | 2 | 3 | 4 | 5 |
| 4. Following directions | 1 | 2 | 3 | 4 | 5 |
| 5. Clean-up | 1 | 2 | 3 | 4 | 5 |
| 6. Overall performance | 1 | 2 | 3 | 4 | 5 |

Comments:

**Domain:** Daily Living Skills
**Competency:** 3. Caring for Personal Needs
**Subcompetency:** 10. Dressing Appropriately

# What Should I Wear?

*Academic Components*

Language (Listening)
Language (Oral Expression)

*Types of Activity*

Discussion
Cut/Paste

*Objective*

The student will be able to identify clothing appropriate to a variety of occasions.

*Activity*

1. Conduct a class discussion on acceptable clothing for different circumstances and weather. The teacher presents the situation; the students identify or describe appropriate clothing. The teacher also presents clothing (pictures can be used); students identify occasions when the clothing would be appropriate. Lists can be made by the class on the chalkboard, or individually in notebooks. Include work, social, school, and casual situations. Include clothing for men and women.

2. The students are presented with short stories in which the main characters are involved in several types of situations. (Make up your own simple, humorous stories, if necessary.) The students cut pictures of clothing out of fashion magazines and catalogs to illustrate each scene of the story.

   Note: More advanced writers can write their own stories, then find pictures to illustrate.

   Note: Although lessons on fashion have traditionally been geared toward girls, boys should also learn about appropriate clothing to meet the occasion. Include as many magazines as possible showing young men's fashion.

*Follow-up; Evaluation*

Given three different situations, the student is able to describe clothing appropriate to each.

**Domain:** Daily Living Skills
**Competency:** 3. Caring for Personal Needs
**Subcompetency:** 11. Exhibiting Proper Grooming and Hygiene

# Grooming Products

*Academic Components*

Health
Reading
Language (Oral Expression)
Language (Written
    Expression)

*Types of Activity*

Discussion
Worksheet

*Objective*

The student will become aware of various grooming and hygiene products and their uses.

*Activity*

1. Discuss various grooming and hygiene products and their uses. Include products used for cleaning the body, oral hygiene, hair care, manicure products, etc. Discuss the difference between health and beauty aids. For example, shampoo is necessary for good health; hair spray is for appearance only.

2. Students bring to class examples of various products: labels, empty boxes or containers, or magazine advertisements. The products can be grouped by the body parts for which they are intended and displayed on a bulletin board.

3. Each student is given an evaluation sheet for one or more products. The student reads the information about the product on the label or in the advertisement. (See example.)

*Follow-up; Evaluation*

1. Given a grooming or hygiene product, the student tells the reason for its use and its importance to good health.

2. A further activity would be to have the students write their own advertisements, emphasizing the products' health benefits, rather than emphasizing the appearance of the user.

### Evaluation Form—Grooming/Hygiene Products

Name of Student: _____
Name of Product: _____

Read the label or the directions for using this product. Answer the following questions about the product:

1. For what part of the body is the product intended?

2. What is the reason for using this product?

3. Does the label or advertisement tell you about the use of this product?

4. Is the use of this product primarily for health or beauty?

5. What are the directions for using this product properly?

6. Are there any safety precautions listed?

7. Is this a product everyone should use? Why?
    If not, who should use it?

8. Do you use this product?
    Do you use another brand of this product?

**Domain:** Daily Living Skills
**Competency:** 3. Caring for Personal Needs
**Subcompetency:** 12. Demonstrating Knowledge of Physical Fitness, Nutrition, and Weight Control

# Self-Evaluation—Keeping Physically Fit

*Academic Components*

    Health
    Science
    Language (Written
      Expression)

*Types of Activity*

    Notebook
    Discussion

*Objectives*

1. The student will evaluate his or her physical fitness, including nutritionally balanced meals, amount of exercise, and amount of rest.
2. The student will show improvement in areas of need.

*Activity*

1. Assist the students in preparing a notebook for keeping a daily physical fitness log. Each page should have a section for recording all foods eaten, amount of exercise, and amount of sleep for one day (see example).
2. Contact the parents and enlist their assistance in this activity. The student keeps a daily record for one week. The student lists all foods eaten, activities involving exercise, and amount of sleep each night.
3. Weigh the students at the beginning and end of the week.
4. At the end of the week, review each student's notebook. Discuss ways the student can improve diet, exercise, or rest schedule. Mark the areas where improvement is needed in brightly colored ink.
5. Repeat this activity periodically; every 4 to 6 weeks at first, then every 2 months.

*Follow-up; Evaluation*

    At each self-evaluation period, the student shows improvement in diet, exercise, weight, and/or rest schedules.

**Self-Evaluation—Keeping Physically Fit**

| Name _____ | Date _____ | Weight_____ |
|---|---|---|
| *Foods:* List everything— NO cheating! | *Exercise:* | *Rest:* |
| *Breakfast:* | *At school:* | I went to bed last night at _____ |
| *Lunch:* | *Sports:* | I got up at _____ this morning. |
| *Dinner:* | *Other:* | I slept _____hours. *Rest during the day:* |
| *Snacks:* | | |

**Domain:** Daily Living Skills
**Competency:** 3. Caring for Personal Needs
**Subcompetency:** 13. Demonstrating Knowledge of Common Illness Prevention and Treatment

# Reading Medicine Labels

*Academic Components*

Reading
Language (Vocabulary)
Language (Written or Oral Expression)
Health

*Types of Activity*

Discussion
Small Group

*Objective*

The student will be able to read a medicine label and answer questions about its use, dosage, and precautions.

*Activity*

1. Conduct a class discussion on the use of various prescription and nonprescription drugs. Discuss terms used on labels (e.g., *dosage, expiration, drowsy, refill, precaution, physician*). Discuss wording of the dosage: "4 times daily," "1 every 4 hours," etc.
2. Provide a variety of labels and *empty* medicine bottles (have students bring some from home, too). Include both pre-scription and nonprescription medicines.
3. Working individually or in small groups, the students answer the following questions about medicine:
   (a) Name of medicine?
   (b) Prescription or nonprescription?
   (c) What illnesses or symptoms does it treat?
   (d) What is the dosage?
   (e) When is the expiration date?
   (f) What special precautions are listed?
4. Groups can report back to the class about the medicines assigned.

*Follow-up; Evaluation*

The student correctly answers the above questions for at least three medicines.

**Domain:** Daily Living Skills
**Competency:** 4. Raising Children, Enriching Family Living
**Subcompetency:** 14. Preparing for Adjustment to Marriage

# Responsibility in Marriage

*Academic Components*

Language (Oral Expression)
Language (Listening)

*Types of Activity*

Discussion
Role Play

*Objective*

The student will be able to identify and describe responsibilities in marriage.

*Activity*

1. Conduct a discussion on the responsibilities of each marriage partner. Allow for a variety of responses; roles vary according to culture, economic situation, and family background. Include social, economic, emotional, child-rearing, home management, and communication responsibilities.
2. Present a situation involving marital responsibilities in one or more of the following ways:
   (a) If video cassette recording equip-

ment is available, record situations (positive or negative) from TV shows or movies. Replay short segments in class.

(b) Read to the class from a story (from literature, or your own story).

(c) Role play a situation.

3. In each of the situations presented, one or both of the marriage partners does not follow through on an expected responsibility or does accept responsibility. The class discusses the possible

consequences of each behavior and offers alternatives.

*Follow-up; Evaluation*

1. The student reports on other examples of marital responsibilities from TV, movies, or reading.

2. The student lists and discusses at least three responsibilities of each marriage partner.

**Domain:** Daily Living Skills
**Competency:** 4. Raising Children, Enriching Family Living
**Subcompetency:** 15. Preparing for Raising Children (Physical Care)

# How Much Does a Baby Cost?

*Academic Components*

Language (Oral Expression)
Reading
Math

*Types of Activity*

Discussion
Small Group

*Objectives*

1. The student will list basic items needed for a baby.

2. The student will discuss the economic factors involved in caring for a baby.

*Activity*

1. The class discusses items that must be purchased by a family in preparation for a baby. The teacher or a student can write the list of items on the board. Include furniture, clothing, bedding, diapers (or diaper service), bottles, formula, and baby food.

2. Working in small groups, the students use catalogs to price as many of the items as possible. Find the total amount needed.

3. Discuss the information discovered in the groups about the cost of having a baby.

4. Emphasize to the students that these items consist of only a portion of the

financial responsibilities of the parents. Other costs include medical expenses (before, during, and after the birth of the baby), child care expenses, increase in utilities, possibility of having to move to a larger house or apartment, increasing food and clothing costs as the baby grows, and education.

5. Discuss alternatives to purchasing new items for the baby, especially furniture. Some alternatives are borrowing from family members or friends, or purchasing used items from garage sales or swap meets, through classified ads, or from used furniture stores.

*Follow-up; Evaluation*

1. The student lists at least five major expenses involved in having a baby.

2. The student discusses, in a written paragraph, the financial responsibilities of parenthood.

**Domain:** Daily Living Skills
**Competency:** 4. Raising Children, Enriching Family Living
**Subcompetency:** 16. Preparing for Raising Children (Psychological Care)

# Where to Go for Help

*Academic Components*

Language (Oral Expression)
Language (Written Expression)

*Type of Activity*

Discussion

*School/Community Resource Person*

School Counselor or Psychologist

*Objective*

The student will be able to identify common family problems and ways of dealing with those problems.

*Activity*

1. Discuss the importance of the family's meeting psychological needs of the children as well as physical needs. List some of those needs (such as love, understanding, acceptance, discipline, and physical contact). Discuss problems that can arise if the child's needs are not being met by the family.
2. Since this is a sensitive subject, allow students to ask questions anonymously. Hand out 3″ × 5″ cards to the class and say, "We will be having a guest speaker to answer our questions about where to go for help when we have a family problem. You may write a question about a problem in your own family, the family of someone you know, or a made-up family. Do not use any names."
3. Invite the school counselor or psychologist to the classroom. Move desks or chairs into a circle to promote open discussion. The counselor discusses problems that the students have written on the cards and suggests ways of dealing with these problems and local agencies where families can receive assistance with these problems.
   *Note:* Remember that the classroom is *not* a counseling session.
   *Note:* Inform the parents in advance of this activity. Invite them to be present.
4. Have cards available listing phone numbers for local Hot Lines and agencies.

*Follow-up; Evaluation*

The student lists three common family problems and at least two ways of dealing with each problem.

**Domain:** Daily Living Skills
**Competency:** 4. Raising Children, Enriching Family Living
**Subcompetency:** 17. Practicing Family Safety in the Home

# Reading Labels for Safety

*Academic Components*

Health
Reading
Language (Vocabulary)
Language (Written Expression)

*Objective*

The student will be able to read and understand important information on labels of common household products.

*Activity*

1. Provide the students with various empty containers of household products such as furniture polish, insecticide, detergents, oven cleaner, etc.

*Types of Activity*

Discussion
Worksheet

2. Discuss vocabulary used on labels related to the safe use of the products (*flammable, caution, danger, poison, inhale, induce, physician,* etc.).

3. Assist the students in locating some of these terms on the labels.
4. The students examine the containers and answer questions about the information on the labels (see examples).

**Reading Labels for Safety**

*Toilet Bowl Cleaner*

1. Is this product dangerous if you swallow it? What words tell you so?
2. What should you do if someone you know swallows it?
3. What should you do if you get it in your eyes?
4. What should you do if you get it on your skin?
5. Copy the words that tell you how to dispose of (throw away) the empty bottle.

*Ant and Roach Killer*

1. Can this product catch on fire easily? What words tell you so?
2. How should you hold the can when spraying?
3. What should you do if someone you know swallows it?
4. What should you do if someone inhales (breathes in) it?
5. Copy the words that tell you how to dispose of (throw away) the empty can.

*Follow-up; Evaluation*

Given a packaged household item, the student can indicate orally how to use the product safely, and safety precautions that should be taken.

**Domain:** Daily Living Skills
**Competency:** 5. Buying and Preparing Food
**Subcompetency:** 18. Demonstrating Appropriate Eating Skills

# Good Manners Begin at Home

*Academic Components*

Language (Oral Expression)
Language (Written Expression)

*Types of Activity*

Role Play
Discussion

*Objective*

The student will be able to demonstrate appropriate eating skills at home and in a restaurant.

*Activity*

1. Discuss the need for good table manners. What does eating behavior tell you about another person?

2. Role play a family meal:
   (a) Students volunteer to play the family roles.
   (b) Have dishes available. One of the family members sets the table. Discuss variations for different occasions.
   (c) Students act out a family meal (you may want to combine this with a cooking lesson and have real food).
   (d) The class discusses appropriate and inappropriate behaviors that were demonstrated.

*School/Community Resource Persons*

Parents

3. Role play eating at a restaurant:
   (a) Choose two to four students to play the "diners." Choose others to act as restaurant personnel: hostess or maitre d', waiter or waitress, or cashier.
   (b) Provide a menu. One of the restaurant workers sets the table.
   (c) Role play the meal, including being seated, ordering, being served, eating, clearing the table, paying, and tipping.
   (d) The class discusses appropriate and inappropriate behaviors that were demonstrated.
4. As time permits, repeat either one of the role-playing activities until each

student has had an opportunity to participate at least once.

*Follow-up; Evaluation*

1. The student writes a paragraph about, or discusses with the teacher, table manners at home and in a restaurant.
2. The student demonstrates appropriate manners in a role-play situation.
3. Involve parents in individual evaluations of the students. Work with the parents and students on areas needing improvement.

**Domain:** Daily Living Skills
**Competency:** 5. Buying and Preparing Food
**Subcompetency:** 19. Planning Balanced Meals

# Let's Eat Right

*Academic Components*

Health
Science
Language (Written Expression)
Language (Oral Expression)

*Types of Activity*

Small Group
Discussion

*Objective*

The student will be able to plan one balanced meal (breakfast, lunch, or dinner) for each day of the week.

*Activity*

1. Complete a published nutrition unit or conduct several class discussions on nutritionally balanced meals. Include breakfast, lunch, and dinner.
2. The students work in pairs for this activity. Each pair pretends they are sharing an apartment and are planning the week's meals. They can choose any meal for each of the seven days. The students list sample menus for each day.
   *Examples*
   Monday: Breakfast
     2 Hard-boiled eggs
     Toast
     Orange juice
     Milk

Tuesday: Dinner
  Hamburgers and buns
  Cheese, lettuce, tomato
  Baked beans
  Milk
Wednesday: Lunch
  Peanut butter and jelly sandwich
  Granola bar
  Apple
  Milk
3. One student from each pair reports to the class. The class discusses the nutritional value of each of the meals presented.

*Follow-up; Evaluation*

1. Given a meal (breakfast, lunch, or dinner), the student lists foods included in a nutritionally balanced meal.
2. The students should save their menus for use in the next activity ("Grocery Shopping").

**Domain:** Daily Living Skills
**Competency:** 5. Buying and Preparing Food
**Subcompetency:** 20. Purchasing Food

# Grocery Shopping

*Academic Components*

Health
Reading
Math
Language (Written
    Expression)

*Types of Activity*

Discussion
Worksheet

(This lesson can also be used as a banking activity.)

*Objective*

The student will be able to make wise purchases when shopping for food within a budget.

*Activity*

1. The students refer to the foods listed in "Let's Eat Right" (Subcompetency 19).
2. Discuss comparison shopping for food: weekly specials, different stores, use of store brands, "warehouse" markets, bulk buying, and use of coupons.
3. Using the grocery ads in your local newspaper, have the students locate as many of the listed foods and their prices as they can. Instruct them to compare prices at different stores and prices of different brands of the same product. The foods they wish to purchase are listed on a worksheet (see example) according to food group. Other foods can be included. The total bill should be between $30 and $50. (Allow the use of a calculator to total their purchases.)

Note: Instruct the students to take note of the "fine print" next to some of the prices: per pound, per ½-pound, each, dozen, etc.

*Follow-up; Evaluation*

1. The student's shopping list contains at least four items from each food group.
2. The student's total grocery bill is within the specified budget.

## Grocery Shopping

1. You have just received another paycheck! Endorse your check, fill out your deposit slip, and add the amount to your check register.

2. Today, you are going grocery shopping. Use the newspaper food ads to help you make your shopping list. Your total bill cannot go over $50, and you must spend at least $30. You must include items from each of the four basic food groups.
    Make your grocery list below. Then add all prices to find the total.

3. Write a check to your favorite supermarket for the total amount. Subtract this total from your balance in your check register.

| *Fruits and Vegetables* | *Price* | *Breads and Cereals* | *Price* |
|---|---|---|---|
| *Meat Group* | *Price* | *Milk Group* | *Price* |
| *Other:* | *Price* | | *Price* |
| | | Grand Total | |

**Domain:** Daily Living Skills
**Competency:** 5. Buying and Preparing Food
**Subcompetency:** 21. Preparing Meals
22. Cleaning Food Preparation Areas

# Classroom Cooking

*Academic Components*

Reading
Health
Language (Vocabulary)

*Types of Activity*

Demonstration
Discussion

*Objectives*

1. The student will be able to read and follow directions on a recipe.
2. The student will be able to clean food preparation areas after cooking.

*Note:* Although most instruction in cooking at the junior high level is accomplished in the home economics department, some recipes can be prepared in the special education classroom. Cooking in the resource room is somewhat limited because of time, but it is still possible and beneficial.

*Activity One*

1. Discuss terminology used in recipes.
2. Write one recipe on the chalkboard or poster. Discuss ingredients, procedures, and utensils needed. During the class discussion, make a list of the ingredients and utensils on the board.
3. Supply each student with a different recipe card. On another piece of paper, each student lists the ingredients and utensils needed for the recipe.

*Activity Two*

1. Select a recipe that can be prepared in the classroom. (Use crock pot, toaster oven, or electric skillet.)
2. Have a copy of the recipe available for each student.
3. List the ingredients and utensils needed on the board. Discuss all steps—from preparation to clean-up.
4. Have all "jobs" printed individually on 3" × 5" cards; number them in sequence. Each student is given one or more job cards.

5. The students follow the procedures on the cards. (See recipe example and job cards.)

**Recipes**

*Chili-Cheese Dip*

1 lb. cheese
1 can chili without beans
4 green onions, chopped
1 can chopped green chili peppers

Mix all ingredients in crock-pot.
Cover and cook on low for 2–3 hours.

*Tortilla Chips*

1 package corn tortillas
salad oil
salt

1. Cut tortillas into strips or wedges.
2. Heat oil in electric skillet—about ¼" deep.
3. Place a few strips at a time in hot oil—turn when slightly browned.
4. Remove strips from oil with tongs. Drain on paper towels.
5. Sprinkle with salt.
6. Serve with Chili-Cheese Dip.

*Follow-up; Evaluation*

1. The student lists ingredients and utensils needed for a recipe.
2. The student follows directions in preparing a recipe.
3. The student adequately cleans up after the food preparation.

**Job Cards**—For Chili-Cheese Dip and Tortilla Chips

| Food Preparation | Clean-Up |
|---|---|
| 1. Wash hands with soap!!<br>2. Cut cheese into cubes—place in crock-pot. | 1. Throw away cheese wrapper.<br>2. Wash knife.<br>3. Wipe cutting board with a damp paper towel. |
| 1. Wash hands with soap!!<br>2. Rinse onions with water. Peel off outer skin.<br>3. Chop into pieces about this long: _____<br>Place in crock-pot. | 1. Wrap onion scraps in paper towel—throw away.<br>2. Wash knife.<br>3. Wipe cutting board with a damp paper towel. |
| 1. Wash hands with soap!!<br>2. Open can of chili.<br>Open can of peppers.<br>3. Place ingredients of both cans in crock-pot. Stir. | 1. Throw away cans.<br>2. Rinse can opener—dry.<br>3. Wipe up any spills.<br>4. After eating, and when crock-pot is cool, wash crock-pot. |
| 1. Wash hands with soap!!<br>2. Cut tortillas into strips or wedges. | 1. Throw away tortilla wrapper.<br>2. Wipe up crumbs from cutting board.<br>3. Wash knife. |
| 1. Wash hands with soap!!<br>2. Pour oil into skillet—about ¼″ deep. Turn on to high heat.<br>3. When oil is hot, place a few chips at a time in oil. When slightly brown, turn with tongs.<br>4. Drain on paper towels. | 1. Put lid back on oil bottle.<br>2. Wipe bottle with damp paper towel.<br>3. Wipe up any spilled or splattered oil. |
| 1. Wash hands with soap!!<br>2. Lightly salt chips as they are draining on paper towels.<br>3. When drained, place chips on paper plates. | 1. When skillet is cool, ask the teacher to pour out oil.<br>2. Wash skillet and tongs.<br>3. Throw away paper towels.<br>4. Wipe counter top. |

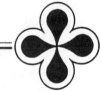

**Domain:** Daily Living Skills
**Competency:** 5. Buying and Preparing Food
**Subcompetency:** 23. Storing Food

# Food Storage

| Academic Components | Objective | Activity |
|---|---|---|
| Health<br>Reading<br>Language (Written Expression)<br>Language (Oral Expression) | The student will identify appropriate storage methods for a variety of foods. | 1. Conduct a class discussion on storing food, including:<br>(a) Where different foods are stored (freezer, refrigerator, cupboard). |

*Types of Activity*

Discussion
Worksheet

(b) Words and phrases to look for on packages indicating proper food storage:
"Refrigerate after opening."
"Store in a cool, dry, place. Do not refrigerate."
"Keep frozen until ready for use. Do not refreeze."
(c) Wrapping and storage containers.
(d) Length of storage.

### Food Storage

| Refrigerator | Freezer | Cupboard |
|---|---|---|
| Milk | Ice cream | Cereal |
| Lettuce—wash and keep in crisper | Hamburger | Crackers |
| | Pizza | Rice |
| Eggs—place in egg tray | Orange juice | |
| Yogurt | | |
| Cheese | | |

(e) Consequences of inappropriately stored food.
2. The students refer to the shopping lists they made in Subcompetency 20: "Grocery Shopping." On another sheet of paper, students group food items according to where they should be stored. Any special handling should be noted. For example, indicate whether or not rewrapping is needed, food should be washed first, or food should be placed in a special section of the refrigerator (see example).
3. The class discusses the individual lists. The students make changes in their own lists, if necessary.

*Follow-up; Evaluation*

Given five different food items, the student indicates the proper method of storage for each.

**Domain:** Daily Living Skills
**Competency:** 6. Buying and Caring for Clothing
**Subcompetency:** 24. Washing Clothing

# Reading Clothing Labels

*Academic Components*

Reading
Language (Written Expression)

*Types of Activity*

Discussion
Small Group
Worksheet

*Objective*

The student will be able to indicate proper washing and drying techniques from clothing labels.

*Activity*

1. Discuss the need for different washing and drying techniques for different fabrics. What are the consequences if the instructions are not carefully followed?
2. Discuss terminology, abbreviations, and illustrations used on clothing care labels.
3. Discuss (and demonstrate) where these labels can be found on different garments.
4. Obtain a variety of labels from a fabric store, or cut them out of old clothing.

5. Working individually or in small groups, the students answer questions about different labels.
(a) Diagrams may be used to indicate washer and dryer settings. (See example.)
(b) Or, students may write responses to questions such as:
(1) At what temperature should you set the washer?
(2) Do you need the dryer? If so, at what setting?
(3) Can you dry clean this garment?

*Follow-up; Evaluation*

Given a care label from a garment, the student will write or discuss how he or she would wash and dry the garment.

**Sample Diagrams for Subcompetencies 24 and 25**

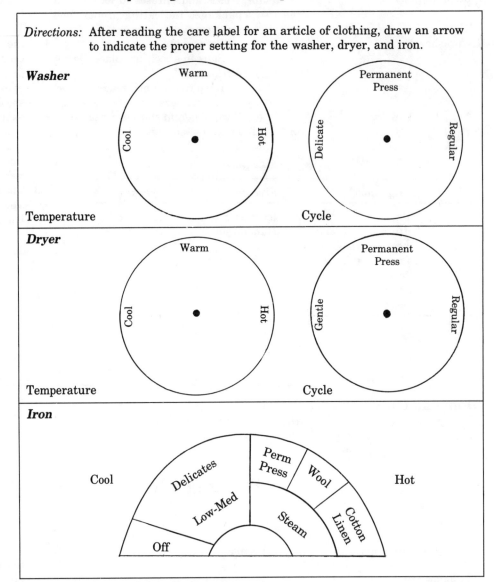

*Directions:* After reading the care label for an article of clothing, draw an arrow to indicate the proper setting for the washer, dryer, and iron.

**Domain:** Daily Living Skills
**Competency:** 6. Buying and Caring for Clothing
**Subcompetency:** 25. Ironing and Storing Clothing

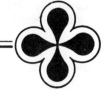

# Ironing Clothing

*Academic Components*

Reading
Language (Oral and Written Expression)

*Objectives*

1. The student will be able to indicate the proper iron setting for a variety of fabrics.

2. The student will demonstrate simple ironing techniques.

*Types of Activity*

Discussion
Worksheet
Demonstration

*Activity*

1. Discuss the need for different iron settings for different fabrics. Include temperature and the use of steam or spray.
2. Using the clothing labels obtained for Subcompetency 24 ("Reading Clothing Labels"), the students (individually or in small groups) indicate iron settings for different fabrics.
   (a) Settings may be indicated on a diagram of a dial (see example for "Reading Clothing Labels").
   (b) Or, students may write responses to questions such as:
      (1) Should you iron this garment?
      (2) What temperature setting for the iron should you use?
      (3) Are there any special ironing instructions for this garment?
3. Use clothing obtained for mending in Subcompetency 26 ("A Stitch in Time Saves Nine"). After the mending activity has been completed, demonstrate simple ironing techniques. Allow the students to practice ironing the garments they have mended.

*Follow-up; Evaluation*

1. Given a care label from a garment, the student writes or discusses how that garment should be ironed.
2. The student demonstrates proper ironing of a simple garment.

**Domain:** Daily Living Skills
**Competency:** 6. Buying and Caring for Clothing
**Subcompetency:** 26. Performing Simple Mending

# A Stitch in Time Saves Nine

*Academic Components*

Visual Perception (Fine Motor)
Language (Oral Expression)
Language (Written Expression)

*Types of Activity*

Demonstration
Discussion

*Objective*

The student will be able to demonstrate various mending techniques for certain types of repairs to clothing.

*Activity*

1. Show the class different articles of clothing that need mending.
2. Demonstrate different mending techniques appropriate to the type of repair needed. Include hand and machine sewing and iron-on patches.
3. Obtain several articles of clothing that need mending. (Students can bring some from home or purchase used clothing at garage sales or thrift shops.) Have at least one article for each student.
4. Students individually analyze each article of clothing and indicate (orally or in writing) which type(s) of mending would be most appropriate.
5. Allow the students to practice hand mending. If a sewing machine and an iron are available for classroom use, allow them to practice mending with the machine and ironing on patches.

*Note:* This activity assumes that the student has the motor skills necessary for hand sewing, and that some basic instruction has already been provided in threading a needle and simple sewing. Some students without previous sewing experience will need extra help from the teacher, aide, or another student.

*Follow-up; Evaluation*

Given a garment in need of repair, the student identifies an appropriate mending technique and performs simple mending.

**Domain:** Daily Living Skills
**Competency:** 6. Buying and Caring for Clothing
**Subcompetency:** 27. Purchasing Clothing

# Planning and Buying a School Wardrobe

*Academic Components*

Reading
Math
Language (Oral Expression)
Language (Written
Expression)

*Types of Activity*

Discussion
Research

*Objective*

The student will be able to plan a basic school wardrobe within a specified budget.

*Activity*

1. Conduct a class discussion on basic clothing items needed for school wear in your area. Include shoes, sweaters, jackets, and underwear in addition to shirts, pants, blouses, skirts, and dresses.
2. Compile a class list of essential items for both boys and girls. Record the list on the board.
3. Each student is assigned a specific amount of money to be used in buying school clothes. (Amounts vary with each student.)
4. Using catalogs and newspaper clothing ads, the students list clothing items and their prices. They must stay within the specified budget. They may not have

money "left over" unless they have purchased all the items agreed upon by the class. (If this lesson is used as part of the Banking unit, each student writes a check to a department store for the total amount of his or her purchases.)
5. Students working with a smaller amount of money will have to shop wisely, and possibly eliminate some items. Students working with a larger amount of money may be able to buy extra clothing.
6. The students share with the class what they discovered about buying clothing within a specified budget.
7. Discuss comparison shopping, sales, and discount stores as a means of saving money when shopping for clothing.

*Follow-up; Evaluation*

The student is within $10 of allotted budget when purchasing school clothing.

**Domain:** Daily Living Skills
**Competency:** 7. Engaging in Civic Activities
**Subcompetency:** 28. Generally Understanding Local Laws and Government

# City Government

*Academic Components*

Social Studies
Language (Oral Expression)
Language (Written
Expression)

*Objectives*

1. The student will be able to identify laws under the jurisdiction of local authorities (city and county).

2. The student will identify the city mayor and some of the city council members.

*Types of Activity*

    Guest Speaker
    Home Involvement
    Class Field Trip

*School/Community Resource Persons*

    Representative from local
       government
    Parents

*Activity*

1. Have a law enforcement officer, lawyer, or judge visit the class to explain local laws. Discuss which types of laws are under local jurisdiction and how they are different from state and federal laws.
2. Assign the students homework to identify the names of their city's mayor and city council members. They may use parents, friends, library, or City Hall as resources.
3. After the students have completed the assignment in exercise 2, briefly discuss the roles of each local official.
4. If possible, visit City Hall to meet the mayor or city council members.

5. If it is not possible to visit City Hall, have the students write letters to the mayor and/or city council. Ask about information on the city government or current local issues. Discuss the replies with the class. The letters can form the basis for a bulletin board on city government. Include pictures of the city officials with their letters.

*Follow-up; Evaluation*

1. The student lists at least three laws under local jurisdiction.
2. The student identifies (orally or in writing) the names of the city mayor and 50% of the city council members.

**Domain:** Daily Living Skills
**Competency:** 7. Engaging in Civic Activities
**Subcompetency:** 29. Generally Understanding Federal Government

# Federal Government

*Academic Components*

    Social Studies
    Reading
    Language (Oral or Written
       Expression)

*Types of Activity*

    Discussion
    Home Involvement
    Bulletin Board

*School/Community Resource Person*

    Parent

*Objectives*

1. The student will be able to identify basic federal laws.
2. The student will identify the President and Vice President of the United States, the Chief Justice of the Supreme Court, and at least one representative of the U.S. Senate or House of Representatives from the local area.

*Note:* A comprehensive unit on the United States Constitution is usually included in social studies classes at the junior high level. The resource or special education teacher should work with the social studies teacher to provide adequate instruction for the special education students in this study area.

*Activity*

1. Conduct a discussion on the types of laws under the jurisdiction of the fed-

eral government. Coordinate this discussion with the social studies teacher's activities on the United States Constitution.
2. Prepare a chart illustrating the three branches of the U.S. government: executive, legislative, and judicial. Use this chart on a bulletin board.
3. Assign the students homework to find out the names of:

    (a) President of the United States
    (b) Vice President of the United States
    (c) Chief Justice of the Supreme Court
    (d) U.S. senators from the state
    (e) Local members of the U.S. House of Representatives

4. After the students have completed the assignment in exercise 2, briefly discuss the roles of each official. Add the names of the government officials to the chart; the students indicate the correct branch of government for each official. Add pictures of each of the officials.

*Follow-up; Evaluation*

1. The student lists at least three laws under federal jurisdiction.
2. The student identifies (orally or in writing) the names of the President of the United States, the Vice President, the Chief Justice of the Supreme Court, and at least one member of the U.S. Senate or House of Representatives from the local area.

**Domain:** Daily Living Skills
**Competency:** 7. Engaging in Civic Activities
**Subcompetency:** 30. Understanding Citizenship Rights and Responsibilities

# Know Your Rights and Responsibilities

*Academic Components*

Social Studies
Reading
Language (Oral Expression)
Language (Written
    Expression)

*Types of Activity*

Discussion
Home Involvement
Notebook
Bulletin Board

*School/Community Resource
    Person*

Parent

*Objective*

The student will be able to identify basic civil rights and responsibilities of citizens.

*Activity*

1. Conduct a class discussion on basic civil rights, especially as related to young people. Include rights of the handicapped. Examples include: rights to education, equal employment opportunities, housing, voting.
2. Discuss the responsibilities of citizenship. Include voting, obeying laws, and paying taxes.
3. Include in the discussions what happens when rights are denied or what happens when citizens do not accept their responsibilities. Relate this to the rights and responsibilities of students and teachers at school.

4. Bring several current newspapers to class. Assist the students in locating articles illustrating:
   (a) Citizens' rights being upheld or denied
   (b) Examples of "good citizenship"
5. Assign the students homework to collect similar newspaper articles over a 2-week period. Inform the parents of this activity so they can offer assistance at home, especially for the less able readers.
6. Compile the newspaper articles in individual "Citizenship" notebooks and/or for use on a bulletin board.

*Follow-up; Evaluation*

The student gives an example (orally or in writing) of at least one civil right and at least one responsibility of citizenship.

**Domain:** Daily Living Skills
**Competency:** 7. Engaging in Civic Activities
**Subcompetency:** 31. Understanding Registration and Voting Procedures

# Voting—A Privilege of Citizenship

*Academic Components*

Social Studies
Language (Vocabulary)
Language (Oral Expression)
Reading
Language (Written
   Expression)

*Types of Activity*

Discussion
Role Play
Notebook

*Objective*

The student will be able to identify requirements for voter registration and voting procedures.

*Activity One*

1. Obtain voting registration forms for classroom use, or make facsimiles. Discuss the requirements for voting in local, state, and national elections. After discussing vocabulary on registration forms, assist the students in filling out the forms.
2. Conduct a class election using as many true-to-life procedures as possible. The students can be vying for actual class offices, or have a mock election for President, Governor, or Mayor.
   (a) Campaigning—discuss the importance of being aware of issues.
   (b) Voting—use sample ballots, or make facsimiles.

(c) Using voting booths—stress the importance of the secret ballot.

*Activity Two*

1. During an election year, study the real candidates and issues:
   (a) Using newspaper articles and campaign materials, the students compile a notebook on one candidate or one issue. Each student reports to the rest of the class.
   (b) Conduct classroom debates on the issues.
2. The students register and vote as in Activity One.

*Follow-up; Evaluation*

The student lists the requirements for voting and basic voting procedures.

**Domain:** Daily Living Skills
**Competency:** 7. Engaging in Civic Activities
**Subcompetency:** 32. Understanding Selective Service Procedures

# Uncle Sam Wants *You!*

*Academic Components*

Social Studies
Language (Oral Expression)

*Objective*

The student will be aware of current draft procedures and will understand the reasons for having a draft.

*Activity*

1. The teacher (or a parent in the military) discusses with the class the reasons for having a draft at different times in American history.

*Types of Activity*

Discussion
Guest Speaker

*School/Community Resource Persons*

Representatives—United States Armed Forces

2. Discuss the current Selective Service procedures:
   (a) Who must register
   (b) When registration must be done
   (c) Where registration can be done
   (d) Penalties for not registering
3. Obtain registration cards from the Post Office or a recruiter to show the students.
4. Invite a representative from a local recruiting office to discuss registration and/or careers in the military services.

*Follow-up; Evaluation*

The student identifies and briefly discusses (orally or in writing) the current Selective Service registration procedures and the reasons for the draft.

**Domain:** Daily Living Skills
**Competency:** 7. Engaging in Civic Activities
**Subcompetency:** 33. Understanding Civil Rights and Responsibilities When Questioned by Representatives of the Law

# Accused of a Crime

*Academic Components*

Social Studies
Language (Oral Expression)
Language (Written Expression)

*Types of Activity*

Role Play
Discussion

*Objective*

The student will identify the basic rights and responsibilities of a citizen when being questioned by the police, as one accused of a crime, and as a witness to a crime.

*Activity*

1. Conduct a class discussion on a citizen's rights when being questioned by representatives of the law, as one accused of a crime, and as a witness to a crime. If possible, have a law enforcement officer speak to the class.
2. Organize a role-playing activity showing a crime being committed. Participating students should be thoroughly instructed in their roles beforehand.
   *Suggested Incident:*
   (a) One or two persons rob a small market.
   (b) Witnesses present: storekeeper, one or two customers in the store, one or two passers-by outside the store.
   (c) One witness contacts the police department.
   (d) Two police officers arrive as the suspects are attempting to get away.
   (e) The suspects are arrested and questioned.
   (f) The witnesses are questioned.
3. Discuss the incident with the class.
   (a) Did the police exercise their responsibilities in arresting the suspects?
   (b) Did any of those questioned have any of their rights denied?
   (c) Did the witnesses behave in a responsible manner?
   (d) What should you do if your rights are denied?
4. Repeat the above incident, or a similar incident. This time, an innocent bystander is arrested and accused of the crime. Discuss with the class.
   *Note:* If you are unable to do role playing such as this with your group of students, a filmed incident or a recorded TV incident can be used instead.

*Follow-up; Evaluation*

The student writes a short paragraph identifying the rights and responsibilities of the police, the accused, and the witnesses in the above incidents.

**Domain:** Daily Living Skills
**Competency:** 8. Utilizing Recreation and Leisure
**Subcompetency:** 34. Participating Actively in Group Activities

# The Importance of Rules

*Academic Components*

Physical Education
Language (Oral Expression)

*Types of Activity*

Game
Discussion
Small Group

*Objective*

The student will learn a new group game and play according to the rules.

*Activity*

1. Conduct a class discussion on the importance of rules when playing a group game. Discuss a familiar game such as baseball:
   (a) What happens if someone wants to play who doesn't know the rules?
   (b) What would happen if one player or team decided to change some of the rules?
   (c) Why are umpires needed in a game like this?
2. Divide the class into two groups. Give each group the rules to a different new game. The teacher can work with one group, and the aide with the other group, to help the students understand the rules to the game. Try the game with the small groups.
3. Bring the class together again. Each group takes a turn teaching the whole class the new game.
4. After playing both new games, discuss with the class:
   (a) Was it easy to learn a new game?
   (b) What was most difficult part following the rules?
   (c) Do you think these games are fun?
   (d) Is it easy or difficult to explain the rules of a new game to someone else?

*Follow-up; Evaluation*

The student demonstrates knowledge of the rules of a new game by playing the game.

**Domain:** Daily Living Skills
**Competency:** 8. Utilizing Recreation and Leisure
**Subcompetency:** 35. Knowing Activities and Available Community Resources

# Bulletin Board—Community Recreation

*Academic Components*

Language (Written
  Expression)
Language (Oral Expression)

*Objective*

The student will report on one community recreational activity.

*Activity*

1. Briefly discuss the availability of recreational facilities in the community. Ask students to discuss activities in

*Types of Activity*

Discussion
Home Involvement
Bulletin Board

*School/Community Resource Persons*

Community Recreation
Personnel

which they have participated.

2. Have a list of facilities, activities, and organizations prepared beforehand. Assign, or allow students to choose, one activity they have not participated in previously. (They may work in pairs.)

3. Assist students in preparing questions they would like answered about the activity. Write the questions on cards.
   *Example:* City Swimming Pool
   (a) What hours is the pool open?
   (b) How much does it cost for children and adults?
   (c) When do you offer swimming lessons?
   (d) Are there any special activities at the pool?

4. Inform the parents of this activity and encourage them to assist the students. The students visit the community facilities to find the information.

5. The students report what they have learned to the class.
   (a) Oral report.
   (b) Written report. All students write a short, neat report including the questions and answers about the activity.
   (c) Bulletin board. Written reports will be placed on a bulletin board along with pictures and brochures from the various facilities and organizations. Include a map of the city with recreational facilities indicated by stars.

*Follow-up; Evaluation*

The student writes a brief report on a recreational facility or organization in the community to be included in a class bulletin board.

---

**Domain:** Daily Living Skills
**Competency:** 8. Utilizing Recreation and Leisure
**Subcompetency:** 36. Understanding Recreational Values

---

## How Do I Use My Time?

*Academic Components*

Health
Physical Education
Language (Oral Expression)
Language (Written Expression)

*Types of Activity*

Discussion
Chart
Home Involvement

*School/Community Resource Person*

Parent

*Objectives*

1. The students will keep records of how they use their time for 1 week (or 1 day).

2. The students will explore ways in which they can positively use their free time.

*Activity*

1. Prepare a daily chart listing all the hours of the day. Have enough copies available for each student for 1 week.

2. Inform the parents ahead of time that the students will be keeping a record of how they use their time in 1 week. Explain the importance of parental assistance.

3. Demonstrate to the students how the charts are to be filled out. The students should list general activities; they should

not get bogged down in details (see examples).

4. The students fill out one chart each day for a week; return each chart to school the next day.
   *Note:* Adapt this activity to the ability of your students. You may want to do this for 1 day, a weekend, or only during school hours.

5. When all charts are completed, the student outlines "leisure time" with a brightly colored pen. Help the students analyze how they are using their leisure time.

6. As a class, discuss how the students can better use their leisure time.

*Follow-up; Evaluation*

1. The student completes a chart of how he or she uses time for at least 1 day

## Example—School Day

Day of the Week: Tuesday

| A.M. | 1:00 | Sleep |
|---|---|---|
| | 2:00 | Sleep |
| | 3:00 | Sleep |
| | 4:00 | Sleep |
| | 5:00 | Sleep |
| | 6:00 | Sleep |
| | 7:00 | Get up, get dressed, walk to school |
| | 8:00 | School |
| | 9:00 | School |
| | 10:00 | School |
| | 11:00 | Lunch |
| Noon | 12:00 | School |
| P.M. | 1:00 | School |
| | 2:00 | Baseball practice |
| | 3:00 | Walk home, get a Coke, watch TV |
| | 4:00 | TV |
| | 5:00 | TV |
| | 6:00 | Dinner |
| | 7:00 | Homework |
| | 8:00 | TV |
| | 9:00 | Take shower, go to bed |
| | 10:00 | Sleep |
| | 11:00 | Sleep |
| Midnight | 12:00 | Sleep |

## Example—Weekend

Day of the Week: Saturday

| A.M. | 1:00 | Sleep |
|---|---|---|
| | 2:00 | Sleep |
| | 3:00 | Sleep |
| | 4:00 | Sleep |
| | 5:00 | Sleep |
| | 6:00 | Sleep |
| | 7:00 | Sleep |
| | 8:00 | Sleep |
| | 9:00 | Get up, eat breakfast, watch TV, get dressed |
| | 10:00 | TV |
| | 11:00 | Play outside |
| Noon | 12:00 | Lunch, get ready for baseball game |
| P.M. | 1:00 | Baseball game |
| | 2:00 | Baseball game |
| | 3:00 | Do chores |
| | 4:00 | Play video games |
| | 5:00 | Go swimming at Chad's house |
| | 6:00 | Swimming |
| | 7:00 | Dinner |
| | 8:00 | Go to movie |
| | 9:00 | Movie |
| | 10:00 | Movie |
| | 11:00 | Go to bed |
| Midnight | 12:00 | Sleep |

and indicates how much of the time is leisure time.

2. The student lists at least two ways in which he or she can better use leisure time.

3. Save the charts for Follow-up to Subcompetency 38 ("Discovering Personal Interests").

**Domain:** Daily Living Skills
**Competency:** 8. Utilizing Recreation and Leisure
**Subcompetency:** 37. Using Recreational Facilities in the Community

## Recreation in (name of city)

*Academic Components*

Health
Physical Education
Language (Oral Expression)

*Types of Activity*

Discussion
Bulletin Board
Home Involvement

*School/Community Resource
Persons*

Parents
Community Recreation
Personnel

*Objective*

The student will keep a record of personal use of community recreational facilities.

*Activity*

1. Prepare a poster listing recreational facilities and organizations in your community. (See Subcompetency 35: "Bulletin Board—Community Recreation.")
2. Weekly, perhaps each Monday, give each student an opportunity to record his or her name and date next to any facilities used during the week. Record participation in organizations such as Scouting, Little League, or church groups.

3. For students who are not participating in any activities, review the previous lessons on the values of positive use of leisure time. If the student does not have any positive leisure time activities, schedule a conference with the parents to jointly identify new ideas.
4. Encourage all students to try new activities occasionally, without over-scheduling their leisure time.

*Follow-up; Evaluation*

The student participates in at least one community recreational activity weekly, and records the participation on a classroom chart.

**Domain:** Daily Living Skills
**Competency:** 8. Utilizing Recreation and Leisure
**Subcompetency:** 38. Planning and Choosing Activities Wisely

## Discovering Personal Interests

*Academic Components*

Reading
Language (Written and
Oral Expression)

*Objective*

The student will evaluate personal interest in the area of leisure time.

*Activity*

1. Administer an interest inventory to the class or individual student. (Use a published inventory or prepare your own.)

## Types of Activity

Worksheet
Discussion
Home Involvement

## School/Community Resource Person

Parent

Sample questions:
(a) Would you rather play baseball or chess?
(b) Would you rather go to the Grand Canyon or Hawaii for a vacation?
(c) Would you rather spend an afternoon by yourself or with friends?
(d) I like to read about _____.
(e) My favorite game is _____.
(f) When I am with my best friend, we like to _____.

2. Discuss each student's inventory individually. Refer to the charts the students made for Subcompetency 36 ("How Do I Use My Free Time?"). Discuss ways in which the student can improve leisure time activities.
3. Include the parents in this activity and encourage development of new leisure time interests for the entire family.

## Follow-up; Evaluation

After a specified time period (4 to 6 weeks), repeat the charts made for Subcompetency 36. Have the student note changes in the use of free time.

**Domain:** Daily Living Skills
**Competency:** 8. Utilizing Recreation and Leisure
**Subcompetency:** 39. Planning Vacations

# Making a Travel Journal

## Academic Components

Reading
Language (Written Expression)
Math

## Types of Activity

Notebook
Home Involvement

## School/Community Resource Person

Parent

### Objective

The student will make a journal to be used on a family vacation.

### Activity

Assist the students in constructing a notebook to be used during the summer on family trips. If the family is not going to be traveling, the notebook can be used to record special activities at home or local points of interest. The notebook will be divided into three main sections. Use a looseleaf notebook with dividers, or make a notebook divided into sections, using heavy paper for the cover.

1. Journal. Have several pages available for students to record special activities, points of interest visited, unusual happenings, etc. Encourage them to write about their experiences: why they enjoyed a certain place, what they learned (gives practice in written English skills).
2. Expenses. The student can keep a record of personal expenses on a trip or for special activities, recording the date, item, and cost. The student keeps a daily or weekly total (gives practice in math skills).

3. Mileage. If the family is traveling, the student can keep track of the number of miles driven daily and gas mileage. Have an example of how to calculate gas mileage in this section (gives practice in math skills). In addition, a large envelope can be attached to the inside back cover of the notebook. The student can use this to collect postcards and information brochures from places visited.

The parents should be involved in this activity. Explain to them how the use of this journal reinforces reading, writing, and mathematical skills, as well as providing an interesting record of summer activities.

### Follow-up; Evaluation

1. The student uses the travel journal on a class field trip. The student makes at least one entry in each section of the notebook.
2. If the student is returning to your class after summer vacation, he or she brings in the travel journal in the Fall and shares it with the class.

**Domain:** Daily Living Skills
**Competency:** 9. Getting around the Community (Mobility)
**Subcompetency:** 40. Demonstrating Knowledge of Traffic Rules and Safety Practices

# Bicycle Safety

*Academic Components*

Social Studies
Reading
Language (Oral Expression)
Art

*Types of Activity*

Discussion
Bulletin Board
Illustration
Class Field Trip

*School/Community Resource Persons*

Police Officer
Automobile Club
Representative

*Objective*

The student will demonstrate knowledge of bicycle safety rules.

*Activity*

The following is a list of suggestions to be used in the classroom promoting bicycle safety:
1. Review traffic signs. Discuss the importance of obeying the signs when riding a bicycle.
2. Discuss the rules made specifically for bicycles, and the reasons for having those rules.
3. Invite a representative from the police department or automobile club to discuss bicycle safety.
4. Decorate the classroom with safety posters and traffic signs.
5. Conduct a poster contest in the classroom. Each student makes a poster illustrating a different bicycle safety rule.
6. Plan a bicycle field trip to a nearby destination. Allow the students to bring their own bikes from home; borrow bikes for those who do not have them.
7. Show the students a film on bicycle safety.

*Follow-up; Evaluation*

The student lists (orally or in writing) at least five rules that should be observed when riding a bicycle.

**Domain:** Daily Living Skills
**Competency:** 9. Getting around the Community (Mobility)
**Subcompetency:** 41. Demonstrating Knowledge and Use of Various Means of Transportation

# Can You Get from Here to There?

*Academic Components*

Reading
Language (Oral Expression)
Language (Listening)

*Objective*

The student will be able to read and understand a street map.

*Activity*

1. As a class project, draw a map showing the school and surrounding neighborhoods. The map should be drawn on a large piece of paper and put on a bulletin board.
   (a) Students write in names of streets.
   (b) Determine where north is on the map and draw a compass.
   (c) Draw local points of interest, for example, park, snack shop, shopping center.
   (d) Students locate and mark their

*Types of Activity*

Bulletin Board
Discussion

homes on the map. They each trace on the map the route they take to get to school. If they take the bus to school, they mark the bus stop and trace the bus route to school. (Since several students may take the same bus, draw the bus route only once.)

2. Practice giving and following directions using this map. Some examples are:
(a) Following directions: Say, "From the school, go east on Trask, turn right on Fairview. Go two blocks more. At which intersection are you?"
(b) Giving directions: Students give oral directions on how to go to their houses. Other students follow the directions by tracing on the map.

*Note*: Allow for ample practice on this activity. It is very difficult for some students, especially those with laterality problems. Give short directions at first, then increase the number of directions.

*Follow-up; Evaluation*

1. Using a map drawn by the class, the student can locate his or her own home.
2. The student can trace a route from one point to another on the map, following oral or written directions.
3. The teacher may transfer this activity to a printed local street map, using the same goals and activities.

**Domain:** Daily Living Skills
**Competency:** 9. Getting around the Community (Mobility)
**Subcompetency:** 42. Driving a Car

# A Town Without Rules

*Academic Components*

Reading
Language (Vocabulary)
Language (Oral Expression)
Language (Written Expression)

*Types of Activity*

Discussion
Composition

*Objectives*

1. The student will become familiar with the Department of Motor Vehicles' Driver's Handbook.
2. The student will understand the importance of traffic signs and rules.

*Activity*

1. Conduct a class discussion on the importance of traffic signs and rules. Discuss specific rules and why we have them. Display pictures of traffic signs; review the familiar ones, and discuss any that may be new to the students. Discuss the importance of using symbols instead of words on some signs. Discuss the consequences of not obeying traffic signs and rules.

2. Obtain several copies of your state's Driver's Handbook from the Department of Motor Vehicles. Use this for reading activities and vocabulary/spelling lessons.
3. Have the students write a paragraph about a town that had no traffic signs or rules. What would happen if drivers were inconsiderate? What would happen if drivers drove carefully anyway? Could they still get in an accident? How would bicyclists and pedestrians be affected?
4. The students can read their compositions to the class, if they choose.

*Follow-up; Evaluation*

Given three traffic rules or signs, the student discusses (orally or in writing) the reasons for having those signs or rules, and the consequences for not obeying them.

# 2. Personal-Social Skills

## Competencies

10. Achieving Self-Awareness
11. Acquiring Self-Confidence
12. Achieving Socially Responsible Behavior
13. Maintaining Good Interpersonal Skills
14. Achieving Independence
15. Achieving Problem-Solving Skills
16. Communicating Adequately with Others

---

**Domain:** Personal-Social Skills
**Competency:** 10. Achieving Self-Awareness
**Subcompetency:** 43. Attaining a Sense of Body

---

## What I Look Like

*Academic Components*

Language (Oral Expression)
Language (Written
Expression)

*Types of Activity*

Discussion
Composition

*Objective*

The student will describe personal physical characteristics, including those considered both positive and negative.

*Activity*

1. Discuss the variations in physical characteristics among students of this age level.
2. The students write a paragraph describing themselves, using the third person. Instruct them to describe themselves as if they were describing someone else, being as honest and as accurate as they can. Include: height; weight; color of eyes; glasses; color, length, and style of hair; freckles; scars.

(a) Collect all compositions and read to the class, omitting the name of the author. The class tries to guess who is being described.
(b) If a student writes an inaccurate description, work with the student privately to gain an accurate personal perception.

*School/Community Resource Persons*

Counselor
Parent

3. Through another written assignment, or a private interview, the students tell what they like about their physical characteristics. They also describe characteristics they would like to change.
4. Discuss with the class individual responses in exercise 3 (for those students who would like to share this information).
   (a) Discuss the differences among characteristics that change by maturation (height, body changes in puberty), characteristics that can be voluntarily changed (hair style, weight), and characteristics that cannot be changed (eye color).
   (b) Assist the students in making decisions and following through on changes they can make to improve appearance (take better care of skin, lose weight).
   (c) Assist the students in finding ways to accept physical characteristics that cannot be changed (physical handicaps, height).
5. Involve parents and the counselor if a student is having a difficult time accurately perceiving personal physical characteristics, or has a severely negative body image.

*Follow-up; Evaluation*

The student lists at least three positive personal physical characteristics, and one physical characteristic he or she would like to change.

**Domain:** Personal-Social Skills
**Competency:** 10. Achieving Self-Awareness
**Subcompetency:** 44. Identifying Interests and Abilities

# Personal Interests and Abilities

*Academic Components*

Reading
Language (Oral Expression)

*Types of Activity*

Discussion
Worksheet

*Objectives*

1. The student will be able to differentiate between interests and abilities.
2. The student will list personal interests and abilities.

*Activity*

1. Discuss the difference between interests and abilities and how they relate to one another. An interest is something you *like* to do; an ability is something you *can* do. Most people usually do a better job at something they are also interested in. Discuss with the students how interests and abilities relate to planning for the future.
2. Write a list of specific interests and abilities on the board. Students orally identify each as an interest or ability, and give reasons for choosing either interest or ability.
3. Students are given a worksheet listing interests and abilities. Students individually write "I" next to words describing interest; "A" next to words describing abilities (see sample worksheet).
4. Students write lists of their own interests and abilities. The teacher and aide should work individually with students on this part of the activity. Adolescents often have difficulty being open about their abilities. They sometimes feel they "can't do anything," or they "can do everything." Point out some abilities they do have to help them be realistic.

## Interests and Abilities

*Directions:* Write "I" next to words describing interests.
Write "A" next to words describing abilities.

_____ like to play baseball
_____ can read well
_____ enjoy building things
_____ play piano
_____ can run fast
_____ can swim well
_____ like to listen to music
_____ like camping
_____ enjoy video games
_____ have good handwriting
_____ spell well
_____ like to cook
_____ can type
_____ like to eat
_____ like to draw
_____ like to go to sports
     events

_____ know how to divide
_____ like to use calculator
_____ can prepare a whole meal
_____ like to play with young children
_____ can play tennis
_____ think reading is fun
_____ like to ride a bicycle
_____ can fix a bike
_____ enjoy going to the beach
_____ watch TV
_____ like playing handball
_____ passed physical fitness test
_____ like to sew
_____ can make a dress
_____ am first string baseball player

*Follow-up; Evaluation*

1. Given a list of phrases, the student differentiates between interests and abilities.
2. The student writes at least five personal interests and five personal abilities.

**Domain:** Personal-Social Skills
**Competency:** 10. Achieving Self-Awareness
**Subcompetency:** 45. Identifying Emotions

# Emotions Inventory

*Academic Components*

Reading
Language (Oral Expression)
Language (Written
   Expression)
Language (Listening)

*Types of Activity*

Discussion
Worksheet

*Objective*

The students will become more aware of their own emotions.

*Activity*

The following sample questions can be used in developing an Emotions Inventory. Administer the inventory to the entire class or to individual students. Privately discuss the inventory with each student.

The responses can be written by the student on a worksheet, or the teacher or aide can read the questions aloud and write the student's oral responses.

1. I feel happy when _____.
2. The most fun I ever had was when _.
3. I worry about _____.
4. When I see two people fighting, I feel _____.
5. When I see two people laughing, I feel _____.
6. I am angry when _____.
7. I get excited about _____.
8. When I see a hurt animal, I feel ____.
9. I hate to _____.
10. I feel hurt when _____.
11. The rain makes me feel _____.
12. I was the most angry when _____.

*School/Community Resource
Person*

Counselor

13. Music makes me feel _____.
14. I cry when _____.
15. I was very sad when _____.
16. I laugh when _____.
17. Love is _____.
18. I am afraid of _____.
19. I feel jealous when _____.
20. The funniest thing I ever saw was __.

*Follow-up; Evaluation*

1. The student completes the Emotions Inventory (orally or in writing).
2. The Inventory can be used to counsel the student privately when needed.
3. Serious emotional problems should be referred to the counselor.

**Domain:** Personal-Social Skills
**Competency:** 10. Achieving Self-Awareness
**Subcompetency:** 46. Identifying Needs

# How We Meet Our Needs

*Academic Components*

Language (Oral Expression)
Health

*Types of Activity*

Discussion
Notebook

*Objective*

The student will identify a variety of ways in which physical and psychological needs can be met.

*Activity*

1. Discuss basic needs (see activities in Competency 4: "Raising Children and Enriching Family Living").
   (a) Physical needs—food, water, clothing, shelter, etc.
   (b) Psychological needs—love, acceptance, security, etc.
2. Discuss different ways in which people meet their needs.
   *Examples*: Need for food can be met by buying food at the grocery store, growing your own food, or eating in a restaurant. The need for love can be met by relationships with family members and relationships with friends.
3. The students make a notebook of different ways in which needs are met. The students may draw pictures for the notebook or cut pictures from magazines. The pictures should depict a physical or psychological need being met. Below each picture, the student should identify the need (or needs) being met in the picture, and whether it is a physical or a psychological need (see examples). This activity may be continued over several days or weeks.

*Follow-up; Evaluation*

Given a physical or psychological need, the student identifies (orally or in writing) at least two ways in which that need can be met.

**Examples—"How We Meet Our Needs" Notebook**

| | | |
|---|---|---|
| (Student-drawn picture of a vegetable garden) | (Magazine picture of a mother hugging her child) | (Photograph of student's family at Thanksgiving dinner) |
| | | Need for food:<br>Physical |
| Need for food:<br>Physical | Need for love:<br>Psychological | Need for love:<br>Psychological |

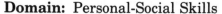

**Domain:** Personal-Social Skills
**Competency:** 10. Achieving Self-Awareness
**Subcompetency:** 47. Understanding the Physical Self

# Sex Education

*Academic Components*

Health
Science

*Type of Activity*

Discussion

*School/Community Resource Persons*

Regular class teacher
Parent

*Objective*

The student will demonstrate knowledge of age-appropriate sexual information.

*Activity*

Instruction on sexual development, reproduction, and related topics is generally conducted in junior high science or health classes, but varies from state to state. The resource specialist usually will not be responsible for teaching this topic, but the special day class teacher might. The following suggestions are methods the resource specialist or special education teacher can use to work with the science teacher in helping the student.

1. If a student is not enrolled in a regular science or health class, talk to the appropriate teacher and parent about placement in a class for the sex education unit (parent permission is required). This involvement in the regular class is valuable, as many excellent films and materials are used.
2. Help the special education student with reading and written assignments.
3. Read tests to the student.

4. Be open to answering questions the students might have about what they have learned in the science class.
5. Have a list of referral services available for students who may come to you with problems.
6. Specific activities can be included in the resource or special education class-

room, in compliance with the district's guidelines.

*Follow-up; Evaluation*

The student completes the district-approved sex education unit.

**Domain:** Personal-Social Skills
**Competency:** 11. Acquiring Self-Confidence
**Subcompetency:** 48. Expressing Feelings of Worth

# "I Can" Game

*Academic Components*

Language (Oral Expression)
Language (Written Expression)

*Type of Activity*

Game

*Objective*

The student will be able to express a positive "I can" statement for a variety of categories.

*Activity*

This is a game that can be played by an entire class, small groups, or two students.
1. Print general ability categories on cards. Examples include Sports, Music, Reading, Getting Along with Others, Math, Making Friends, Art, and Cooking.
2. Playing the game.
   (a) In a group:
      (1) The teacher or a student draws a card and reads the category.
      (2) The students respond by writing (or telling orally) a specified number of "I can" statements (adjust the number of statements required for the specific group of students). In the beginning, require only one or two statements per category. Some students will be able to work up to at least five.
      (3) Repeat as often as desired.
      (4) Use of points for number of responses is optional.
      (5) If a few students are doing all the responding, call on students

by name or take turns around the circle.
   (b) For two players: The students alternate reading cards and giving responses.
   (c) Variation: As the students progress in this game, require the "I can" statements to reflect something that the student could not do last year (or last month or week) but can do now.

*Examples*

SPORTS:  I can hit a baseball.
         I can run.
         I can play ping-pong.
         I can do 20 sit-ups.
GETTING ALONG WITH OTHERS:
         I can follow directions.
         I can be friendly.
         I can help others.
         I can follow school rules.
*Note*: "I can" statements must be positive and realistic. Unacceptable responses: I can hit my brother, I can jump off the building.

*Follow-up; Evaluation*

Given a general ability category, the student responds (orally or in writing) with at least (*number*) positive, realistic "I can" statements.

**Domain:** Personal-Social Skills
**Competency:** 11. Acquiring Self-Confidence
**Subcompetency:** 49. Telling How Others See Him/Her

# He Can/She Can

*Academic Components*

Language (Oral Expression)
Language (Listening)

*Type of Activity*

Game

*Objective*

The student will be able to make realistic, positive statements about a peer's abilities.

*Activity*

This is an adaptation of the "I Can" game (see Subcompetency 48).
1. The students sit in a circle.
2. One student draws a category card and reads the category to the group.
3. Going around the circle, each student responds with a "He Can" or "She Can" statement about the student holding the card. (The statement must be positive and realistic.)
4. The next student draws a card and the exercise is repeated.
5. Optional: Have the students tell how they felt when the others made positive statements about them.

*Follow-up; Evaluation*

Given a general ability category, the student responds with at least one positive, realistic "He Can" or "She Can" statement about a peer.

**Domain:** Personal-Social Skills
**Competency:** 11. Acquiring Self-Confidence
**Subcompetency:** 50. Accepting Praise
                      51. Accepting Criticism

# Is It Praise or Criticism?

*Academic Components*

Language (Oral Expression)
Reading

*Types of Activity*

Discussion
Worksheet

*Objective*

The student will differentiate among statements of praise, criticism, and neutral statements.

*Activity*

1. Conduct a class discussion on praise and criticism. Discuss various ways people praise and criticize others. (Verbally, facial expressions, body language, etc.)
2. Give examples of verbal statements of praise and criticism. Include some statements that are neutral.
3. Have students complete a worksheet. List several phrases or sentences on the worksheet. Students write "P" if it is a praise statement, "C" if it is criticism, and "N" if the statement is neutral (see example).

---

**Is It Praise or Criticism?**

Read the statements below. Next to each statement, write "P" if it shows praise, "C" if it shows criticism, and "N" if it is neither praise nor criticism.

_____ 1. You are doing a good job.
_____ 2. No, that's not right.
_____ 3. I can't read your paper when it's this messy!
_____ 4. I like this story you wrote.
_____ 5. Your story was about football.
_____ 6. Can't you ever keep your room clean?
_____ 7. I like your hair like that.
_____ 8. I'm proud of you!
_____ 9. I wish you would get good grades like your sister.
_____ 10. Your jacket is in the science room.
_____ 11. What a great hit!
_____ 12. I knew you could do it!
_____ 13. You cut this out all wrong.
_____ 14. This is a very neat paper.
_____ 15. John got an "A" on the test.
_____ 16. Your handwriting has really improved.
_____ 17. You didn't follow directions. You have to do this over.
_____ 18. This is a delicious pie you made!
_____ 19. You didn't do your homework *again*?
_____ 20. I like you!

4. Discuss the students' responses with the class.

*Follow-up; Evaluation*

The student correctly responds to at least 80% of the statements on the worksheet.

---

**Domain:** Personal-Social Skills
**Competency:** 11. Acquiring Self-Confidence
**Subcompetency:** 50. Accepting Praise
51. Accepting Criticism

---

# Accepting Praise and Criticism

*Academic Components*

Language (Oral Expression)
Language (Listening)

*Type of Activity*

Discussion

*Objective*

The student will be able to verbalize responses to statements of praise and criticism.

*Activity*

Use the worksheet from the previous lesson ("Is It Praise or Criticism?") in this activity.
1. Read each statement on the worksheet, one at a time.
2. Have the students take turns offering possible verbal responses to each statement (elicit at least two responses for each statement).
3. Discuss the appropriateness of each response.
4. If students are unable to offer an appropriate response to one of the statements, offer suggestions.

*Follow-up; Evaluation*

When presented with a statement involving praise or criticism, the student makes at least one appropriate response.

**Domain:** Personal-Social Skills
**Competency:** 11. Acquiring Self-Confidence
**Subcompetency:** 52. Developing Self-Confidence

# Self-Evaluation

*Academic Component*

Reading

*Type of Activity*

Chart

*Objective*

The students will evaluate themselves on a number of school-related behaviors.

*Activity*

1. Have the students evaluate themselves on their performance on school-related behaviors: coming to school every day on time, bringing a pencil to class, turning in homework on time, etc. The students fill out a chart (see "Self-Evaluation #1") by checking "always," "usually," "sometimes," or "never" next to each behavior. Collect the charts.
2. The students keep weekly charts, recording their actual behaviors listed on "Self-Evaluation #1" (See "Self-Evaluation #2"). Encourage the students to be honest!

3. At the end of 2 weeks, have the students compare the two charts to see if they accurately evaluated their actual performance.
4. Work with students individually on areas where improvement is needed.
5. Offer praise for good performance and improvement.
6. This activity can be continued for a few weeks or for an entire semester.
7. At the end of the entire activity, the students again fill out "Self-Evaluation #1," and compare with the original evaluation, noting improvements.

*Follow-up; Evaluation*

The student keeps a weekly chart on performance at school and shows improvements where needed.

---

*Self-Evaluation # 1*            Name _____

| How do you rate yourself in the following areas? Put a (√) to tell how often you: | Always | Usually | Sometimes | Never |
|---|---|---|---|---|
| 1. Come to school every day | | | | |
| 2. Come to school on time | | | | |
| 3. Bring a pencil to class | | | | |
| 4. Turn in homework on time | | | | |
| 5. Finish classwork on time | | | | |
| 6. Get along with students* | | | | |
| 7. Get along with teachers* | | | | |

*Self-Evaluation #2*            Name _____

| Put a (√) each day you: | *Mon.* | *Tues.* | *Wed.* | *Thurs.* | *Fri.* |
|---|---|---|---|---|---|
| 1. Come to school | | | | | |
| 2. Come to school on time | | | | | |
| 3. Bring a pencil to class | | | | | |
| 4. Turn in homework on time | | | | | |
| 5. Finish classwork on time | | | | | |
| 6. Get along with students* | | | | | |
| 7. Get along with teachers* | | | | | |

*Determined by following class and school rules. No problems with talking inappropriately, name calling, etc.

**Domain:** Personal-Social Skills
**Competency:** 12. Achieving Socially Responsible Behavior
**Subcompetency:** 53. Knowing Character Traits Needed for Acceptance

# Character Traits of Self and Others

*Academic Components*

Language (Oral Expression)
Language (Vocabulary)
Language (Written
Expression)

*Types of Activity*

Discussion
Small Group

*Objective*

The student will become aware of positive character traits in self and classmates.

*Activity*

1. Discuss positive character traits that are needed for acceptance in society. Examples include: cooperation, dependability, friendliness, honesty, etc.
2. Discuss and chart character traits of famous people with which the students are familiar. Discuss how positive character traits helped this person meet his or her goals. A similar activity could include workers in school, successful persons in the community, characters in books or TV.
3. Have the students work in pairs. Each student makes two lists:
   (a) Positive character traits of partner.
   (b) Positive character traits of self.
   (The teacher and aide can circulate during this activity and give assistance where needed.)
4. Each pair of students compares lists. Did they list similar character traits in themselves and each other?

*Follow-up; Evaluation*

The student lists at least five positive character traits in himself or herself and a classmate.

**Domain:** Personal-Social Skills
**Competency:** 12. Achieving Socially Responsible Behavior
**Subcompetency:** 54. Knowing Proper Behavior in Public Places

# Ordering and Paying for Meals in a Restaurant

*Academic Component*

Language (Oral Expression)

*Types of Activity*

Discussion
Role Play

*Objective*

The student will demonstrate proper behavior when ordering and paying for food in different types of restaurants.

*Activity*

1. Discuss behavior and appropriate dress for different types of restaurants (fast-food, coffee shop, etc.). Discuss behavior for each of the following steps: waiting to be seated, reading the menu, making a selection, ordering, eating, paying, and tipping.

| Tip Chart | |
|---|---|
| *Amount of Bill* | *15% Tip* |
| $ 1.00 | $ .15 |
| 2.00 | .30 |
| 4.00 | .60 |
| 5.00 | .75 |
| 7.00 | 1.05 |
| 8.00 | 1.20 |
| 9.00 | 1.35 |
| 10.00 | 1.50 |
| 12.50 | 1.90 |
| 15.00 | 2.25 |
| 17.50 | 2.60 |
| 20.00 | 3.00 |
| 25.00 | 3.75 |
| 30.00 | 4.50 |

2. Have menus available from several different types of restaurants. Allow the students to look through the menus and practice making selections.

3. Have the students take turns role playing eating in different types of restaurants. Give them the following instructions:

(a) Fast-food
(1) Wait in line, if necessary.
(2) Read the menu (usually on the wall) and make your selection before it's your turn to order.
(3) Order clearly and politely.
(4) Have money ready to pay the cashier.
(5) Carry tray of food to the table and eat politely—no loud talking.
(6) Clear the table when finished; throw trash away.
(7) Tipping not necessary.

(b) Coffee shop
(1) Look for a sign that may say, "Please seat yourself" or "Please wait to be seated."
(2) Read the menu and be ready to order when the waiter or waitress comes. If you are not ready, politely ask if he or she can come back in a few minutes.
(3) Know what you want when ordering. Speak clearly and politely.
(4) Show good table manners when eating.
(5) You will usually pay the cashier at a coffee shop.
(6) Leave a tip on the table before you leave. (Discuss how to figure a 15% tip. Students can make a tip chart—see example).

(7) Do not leave the table in a mess. The bus boy or server will clear the table, but they should not have to clean up your sloppiness!

(c) Restaurant
(1) Always wait for the hostess or maitre d' to seat you.
(2) Read the menu carefully. Many restaurants list items a la carte—you will have to pay extra for a salad, for example. Remember this when you get ready to order. (Don't get stuck with ordering more food than you have money for!)
(3) Be prepared and order clearly and politely.
(4) Remember your very best table manners. You will probably be eating on dishes and a tablecloth and using cloth napkins. You may have more than one fork and one spoon. Don't get so uptight that you don't enjoy your meal, though!
(5) The waiter or waitress will probably give you the bill on a little tray or dish. Put your money on the tray. He or she will bring you your change.
(6) Leave your tip on the tray. If you have had outstanding service, you may want to leave more than a 15% tip.
(7) Fold your napkin and place it on the table when you leave.

*Follow-up; Evaluation*

The teacher records demonstration of appropriate behaviors on a chart (see example). The student demonstrates appropriate behaviors at least 80% of the time.

**Evaluation of Appropriate Behaviors**

| Behavior | Always | Sometimes | Never | |
|---|---|---|---|---|
| Order clearly and politely | | | | |
| Demonstrate good table manners | | | | |
| Leave eating area neat | | | | |
| | | | | |

**Domain:** Personal-Social Skills
**Competency:** 12. Achieving Socially Responsible Behavior
**Subcompetency:** 55. Developing Respect for the Rights and Property of Others

# Please Accept My Apology

*Academic Components*

Language (Oral Expression)
Language (Listening)

*Types of Activity*

Discussion
Role Play

*Objective*

The student will demonstrate appropriate ways to apologize and accept an apology.

*Activity*

1. Discuss reasons why we should apologize when we have violated the rights and/or property of others.
2. Prepare several 3″ × 5″ cards for role playing activity. On each card, write an incident involving two people. In each incident, one person's rights have been violated or property damaged, and the other person must offer an apology (see examples).
3. Choose two students at a time to participate. Read the incident on one of the cards. One student acts out apologizing, and the other students acts out accepting the apology. Repeat this activity, with students reversing roles.
4. The class discusses each incident and observes whether or not the apology and acceptance were appropriate.
5. Repeat with another two students.

*Follow-up; Evaluation*

Given a situation where an apology is necessary, the student demonstrates, by role playing, an appropriate way to apologize or to accept an apology.

**Apology Cards**

1. You borrowed your friend's bicycle, rode over some glass, and now his bike has a flat tire.
   Roles: Two friends
2. Your sister loaned you her best necklace to wear to the Spring Dance. You lost it.
   Roles: Two sisters
3. You dropped a library book in a huge mud puddle.
   Roles: Student and librarian
4. You hit a baseball through the neighbor's window.
   Roles: Student and adult neighbor
5. While babysitting, you broke a dish.
   Roles: Teenage babysitter and adult
6. You used your teacher's pen and forgot to return it. Someone took it out of your back pocket at lunch.
   Roles: Student and teacher

**Domain:** Personal-Social Skills
**Competency:** 12. Achieving Socially Responsible Behavior
**Subcompetency:** 56. Recognizing Authority and Following Directions

# Following Directions at School and at Work

*Academic Components*

Language (Oral Expression)
Language (Written
Expression)

*Type of Activity*

Discussion

*Objective*

The student will recognize the difference between the consequences of not following directions at school and at work.

*Activity*

1. Discuss ways in which school rules relate to rules at work. Discuss authority figures who must be obeyed at school (teacher, principal) and at work (boss or supervisor).
2. List on the board ways in which school and work are similar:
   (a) Attendance
   (b) Being on time
   (c) Completing assignments
   (d) Getting along with others
   (e) Respect for authority
   (f) Trying to do a good job
   (g) Asking for help
3. For each category, elicit responses (oral or written) from the students as to how they are different at school and at work, especially the consequences if rules are not followed. For example:
   (a) Attendance—If we miss school too often, our grades will go down, and we may get into trouble with teach-

ers, parents, and the principal. If we miss work too often, we may get fired or not make as much money.
   (b) Being on time—similar to attendance.
   (c) Completing assignments—In school, our grades go down if we don't work and the teacher may keep us after school, but we won't get kicked out. If we don't do our work on the job, we may get fired.
   (d) Asking for help—The teacher is usually around to answer questions. At work, we must listen carefully to instructions the first time and not keep "bugging" the boss. (But don't be afraid to ask if you don't understand.)
4. Stress the importance of practicing appropriate behaviors in school, so they become habits before the students begin working on a job.

*Follow-up; Evaluation*

Given a behavior that is relevant to both school and work, the student gives at least one example (orally or written) for each difference.

**Domain:** Personal-Social Skills
**Competency:** 12. Achieving Socially Responsible Behavior
**Subcompetency:** 57. Recognizing Personal Roles

# Personal Roles

*Academic Components*

Language (Oral Expression)
Language (Written
Expression)

*Types of Activity*

Discussion
Small Group

*Objectives*

1. The student will recognize present and possible future personal roles.
2. The student will identify personal expectations in various roles and how others are affected if those expectations are not met.

*Activity*

1. Define "role." Discuss with the students how a person's role changes in different situations and at different times of life. Give several examples.
2. Have the students list all present personal roles they can think of: son or daughter, friend, student, team member, and so forth.
3. Have the students list several future roles they might have: husband or wife, parent, worker, etc.
4. Discuss the student's lists. Which roles will change as the student grows older, and which will remain the same?
5. In small groups, discuss expectations of each of the roles the students listed. For example:
   (a) Student—expected to come to school, do assigned work, listen to the teacher, follow school rules, etc.
   (b) Friend—expected to listen, be honest, be friendly, help when needed, etc.
6. Using the same roles, discuss how other people are affected if role expectations are not met. For example:
   (a) Student—parents will be disappointed and possibly angry, teacher will be disappointed, etc.
   (b) Friend—others will be hurt, they will refuse to be with you, etc.

*Follow-up; Evaluation*

1. The student lists at least five present roles and at least five possible future roles.
2. The student lists role expectations and describes their effects on others.

**Domain:** Personal-Social Skills
**Competency:** 13. Maintaining Good Interpersonal Skills
**Subcompetency:** 58. Knowing How to Listen and Respond
Listening on the Job

# Ways We Respond

*Objectives*

1. The student will become aware of the importance of good listening skills in a variety of occupations.
2. The student will become aware of different means of response in personal relationships and on the job.

*Academic Components*

Language (Oral Expression)
Language (Listening)
Language (Written
 Expression)

*Type of Activity*

Discussion

*Activity One*

1. Discuss the importance of listening.
2. With the class, compile a list of occupations in which doing a job depends on good listening skills (other than receiving instructions from the supervisor). Write each response on the board. Some examples are:

   reporter
   teacher
   sales clerk
   waiter/waitress
   doctor/nurse
   policeman
   telephone operator
   secretary
   counselor
   receptionist

3. Discuss what might happen if someone who had one of these jobs was not a good listener.

*Activity Two*

1. With the students, compile a list of different ways people respond to each other. Write the list on the board. Some examples are:

   talking
   writing
   typing
   facial expressions
   touching
   gestures

2. Discuss: How do people who are deaf or hearing impaired listen and respond to another deaf person and to a hearing person?
3. Refer to the list of occupations from Activity One. Discuss:
   (a) Do you think a deaf or hearing impaired person could have one of these jobs that require good listening skills? Why or why not?
   (b) How do you think deaf people listen and respond at work?

*Follow-up; Evaluation*

1. Given an occupation, the student tells (orally or written) why good listening skills are important on that job.
2. The student lists at least four ways in which people respond to each other.

**Domain:** Personal-Social Skills
**Competency:** 13. Maintaining Good Interpersonal Skills
**Subcompetency:** 59. Knowing How to Make and Maintain Friendships

# A Friend in Need

*Academic Components*

Language (Oral Expression)
Language (Listening)

*Types of Activity*

Role Play
Discussion

*Objective*

The student will be able to list rights and responsibilities involved in friendship.

*Activity*

1. Have situations printed on 3″ × 5″ cards involving interactions between friends. Include problems, the need for support,

sharing accomplishments, etc. Some examples are:
(a) Your best friend has just broken up with a girlfriend/boyfriend.
(b) Your best friend just learned that his/her parents are getting a divorce.
(c) Your best friend just won a school contest.
(d) Your best friend made the athletic team and you didn't.
(e) Your best friend was not invited to a special party, but you were.

2. Have the students role play situations in pairs. Give each pair a card. They act out what they think is the most appropriate way to respond.
3. The class discusses the situations and suggests alternative responses, if necessary. Discuss the importance of rights and responsibilities involved in friendship.

*Follow-up; Evaluation*

Given a situation involving friendship, the student lists appropriate responses indicating rights and/or responsibilities of friendship.

**Domain:** Personal-Social Skills
**Competency:** 13. Maintaining Good Interpersonal Skills
**Subcompetency:** 60. Establishing Appropriate Heterosexual Relationships

# My Ideal Date

*Academic Components*

Language (Oral Expression)
Language (Written Expression)

*Types of Activity*

Discussion
Worksheet

*Objective*

The student will list qualities he or she would like in a heterosexual dating partner.

*Activity*

1. The students complete a worksheet on "My Ideal Date" (see examples). The students write qualities (not names) they would like in a date on the "clouds."

2. Discuss the responses with the class. List on the board qualities that were similar and different in the individual responses.
3. Discuss reasons why some responses were the same or different.
4. Discuss whether responses were realistic or not.

*Follow-up; Evaluation*

The student lists at least five qualities he or she would like in a date.

BOYS

GIRLS

**Domain:** Personal-Social Skills
**Competency:** 13. Maintaining Good Interpersonal Skills
**Subcompetency:** 61. Knowing How to Establish Close Relationships

# Close to You

*Academic Components*

Language (Oral Expression)
Language (Vocabulary)
Language (Written Expression)

*Types of Activity*

Discussion
Composition
Worksheet

*Objectives*

1. The student will be able to identify and list characteristics of close relationships.
2. The student will be able to identify close relationships in his or her own life, and others with whom he or she could develop a close relationship.

*Activity*

Have several photographs available showing people interacting in different situations. Include parents/children, husband/wife (all ages), siblings, good friends, casual acquaintances, and business colleagues.

1. Show the students the pictures and have them identify the ones that portray people in close relationships.
2. Discuss the pictures that the students chose. List characteristics of close relationships (trust, honesty, acceptance, love, etc.).

3. Each student chooses one picture. The student writes a paragraph telling a story about the people in the picture.
4. The student fills out an activity sheet (see example) listing:
   (a) Present close relationships
   (b) Why those close relationships are important
   (c) Possible close relationships
   (d) Why those relationships might be important

*Follow-up; Evaluation*

1. The student identifies at least three close relationships and at least three characteristics of a close relationship.
2. The student completes the activity sheet listing at least two persons in each category.
3. Several weeks later, review the activity sheets. Has the student developed any additional close relationships?

### Close to You

| I am close to: | Because: |
|---|---|
|  |  |
| I would like to be close to: | Because: |
|  |  |

**Domain:** Personal-Social Skills
**Competency:** 14. Achieving Independence
**Subcompetency:** 62. Understanding Impact of Behavior upon Others

# What's Buggin' You?

*Academic Components*

Language (Oral Expression)
Language (Written
  Expression)

*Types of Activity*

Discussion
Worksheet

*School/Community Resource
  Person*

Counselor

*Objectives*

1. The student will be able to identify behaviors of others that bother him or her.
2. The student will be able to list positive behaviors to replace negative behaviors.

*Activity One*

1. Briefly discuss how the behavior of others affects each of us.

2. Prepare a worksheet showing an outline of a VW "bug," containing several response lines (see example). The students fill in the worksheet with behaviors of others that "bug" them. Stress behaviors, rather than situations or individuals.
3. Have the class group their chairs in a circle. The students read (or discuss) their responses. The teacher should guide the discussion to revolve around behaviors of others, not specific individuals.

**VW "Bug"**
**Elementary and Junior High Worksheet**

# How Not to Be a Bug

*Activity Two*

1. The teacher compiles a list of negative behaviors that "bug" others from the student responses in Activity 1.
2. Conduct one of the following activities:
   (a) List the negative behaviors on the board. As a group, discuss and list appropriate behaviors that would not "bug" others to replace the ones that do.
   (b) Prepare a list of negative behaviors on a worksheet. The students individually list appropriate behaviors that would not "bug" them to replace the ones that do.

*Follow-up; Evaluation*

1. The student identifies and lists at least five behaviors of others that "bug" him or her.
2. The student lists at least five behaviors that would not "bug" him or her.
3. The teacher or counselor can use these responses with individual students to guide them to a realization of personal behaviors that may bother others. The teacher/counselor and students can discuss ways in which students can change behavior so they will not be a "bug" to others.

**Domain:** Personal-Social Skills
**Competency:** 14. Achieving Independence
**Subcompetency:** 63. Understanding Self-Organization

# Organizing Class Time

*Academic Components*

All Academic Areas
Reading
Language (Written Expression)

*Type of Activity*

Chart

*Objective*

Given a list of class assignments (at their level), to be completed within one week, students will be able to budget their class time and complete all assignments.

*Activity*

1. Weekly assignments in a specific subject area are given to the students each Monday. Each assignment should take one class period and should be at the student's instructional level (see example #1).
2. Initially, label each activity with the day it should be completed.
3. When the students have demonstrated competency in completion of assigned daily tasks, allow them to plan their own week, including all assignments given. The students check off assignments as they are completed. The completion of the assignments is verified by the teacher or the aide.
4. Many exceptional students have great difficulty in budgeting time and completing assignments. For these students, the teacher may want to include another sheet on which the student (with assistance, if necessary) lists specific activities completed at the end of each class period (see example #2).

*Follow-up; Evaluation*

The teacher records assignments completed and determines whether the student has demonstrated a level of success in budgeting class time and completing weekly assignments.

**Example 1**

## Weekly Assignment Sheets

| | |
|---|---|
| *Reading Assignments for* _____ (name) _____ *Week of* _____ | |

SRA Kit
Multiple Skills *Book C, #11-15*
Workbook *pp. 63-68*
Book *Read 2 chapters*
Worksheets
Group Lesson *Careers — on Thursday*
Tape Lesson *DLM #10*
Language Master

| | |
|---|---|
| *English Assignments for* _____ (name) _____ *Week of* _____ | |

Spelling *Book 2, Lesson #8*
Workbook *pp. 80-84*
Worksheets *Punctuation*
Composition *Wednesday — "Inventions"*
Group Lesson *Tuesday - review verbs*

| | |
|---|---|
| *Math Assignments for* _____ (name) _____ *Week of* _____ | |

Worksheets *× 16-18; ÷ 5-6*
Workbook *Fractions pp. 8-12*
Flash Cards *Review ÷ facts*
Group Lesson *Banking (Monday)*

**Example 2**

## Record of Daily Assignments

| | Reading | Math |
|---|---|---|
| Monday | Read ½ story | 5 division problems |
| Tuesday | Finished story did 2 questions | 2 division problems Talked to Bill |
| Wednesday | | |
| Thursday | | |
| Friday | | |

**Domain:** Personal-Social Skills
**Competency:** 14. Achieving Independence
**Subcompetency:** 64. Developing Goal-Seeking Behavior

# A Letter to Myself

*Academic Components*

Language (Oral Expression)
Language (Written
Expression)

*Types of Activity*

Discussion
Composition

*Objective*

The student will be able to list personal goals and discuss the achievement of those goals.

*Activity*

1. Discuss goals with the class. Have the students tell their perceptions of what goals are. Discuss the difference between immediate and long-range goals (passing the next science test versus getting a "B" in science on the next report card).
2. At the beginning of the school year, or at New Year's, each student writes a letter to herself, listing personal goals for that semester or year. Immediate and long-range goals should be included. (The students can dictate the letters to the teacher or aide.)
3. Each student's letter is sealed in an envelope, and addressed to himself. The teacher saves the letters, to be mailed

or given to the students at the end of a set period.
4. When the students receive the letters at the end of the semester or year, they check off the goals that have been met. Discuss the following with each student:
   (a) What did you do to meet the goals?
   (b) Why do you think you did not meet some of the goals? Not enough time? Didn't try? Unrealistic goal? Poor planning? Barrier because of handicap?
   (c) For realistic goals that have not been met, assist the student in developing a plan for meeting those goals.

*Follow-up; Evaluation*

1. The student lists at least five realistic personal goals.
2. After a specified period of time, the student discusses why he or she did or did not achieve goals.

**Domain:** Personal-Social Skills
**Competency:** 14. Achieving Independence
**Subcompetency:** 65. Striving toward Self-Actualization

# Are You Doing the Best You Can?

*Academic Components*

Language (Oral Expression)
Reading

*Objective*

The student will evaluate effort in school-related tasks.

*Activity*

1. Discuss with the students the value of effort and persistence in achieving goals.

*Types of Activity*

Discussion
Worksheet

Relate this to tasks at school. Emphasize the importance of doing your best, regardless of the performance of others.

2. Give each student an evaluation sheet (see example). Instruct the students to answer each question with "Yes" or "No" for each task.

3. Discuss student responses individually. Assist the student to develop realistic goals in areas where improvement is needed. Praise the student for "doing the best you can."

*Follow-up; Evaluation*

1. The student realistically evaluates effort on school-related tasks by completing an evaluation sheet.

2. The student discusses and sets goals for tasks where improvement is needed.

**Are You Doing the Best You Can?**

Answer each question with "yes" or "no."

Do you think you can do this . . .

|  | *Better than your classmates?* | *About the same as your classmates?* | *Not as well as your classmates?* | *Are you doing the best you can?* |
|---|---|---|---|---|
| Reading |  |  |  |  |
| Spelling |  |  |  |  |
| Writing |  |  |  |  |
| Addition |  |  |  |  |
| Multiplication |  |  |  |  |
| Subtraction |  |  |  |  |
| Division |  |  |  |  |
| Listening |  |  |  |  |
| Speaking |  |  |  |  |
| Art |  |  |  |  |
| Music |  |  |  |  |
| P.E. |  |  |  |  |

**Domain:** Personal-Social Skills
**Competency:** 15. Achieving Problem-Solving Skills
**Subcompetency:** 66. Differentiating Bipolar Concepts

# The Best Thing to Do/The Worst Thing to Do

*Academic Components*

Language (Listening)
Language (Oral and
Written Expression)

*Objective*

The student will be able to identify positive and negative consequences of behaviors in a problem situation.

*Activity*

1. Present problem situations to the class (depicted in pictures or written on cards). Examples:

*Types of Activity*

Discussion
Worksheet

Two students are in a store. One of the students pockets some merchandise.
A student finds a piece of jewelry that looks very expensive.
One student asks another to help him cheat on a test.
A student finds a lost child in a busy shopping center.

2. Discuss both positive and negative behaviors and their consequences for each situation. Record student responses on a chart on the board, or provide each student with a worksheet to record his or her own responses (see example). Try to discover one best and one worst thing to do in each situation.

*Follow-up; Evaluation*

The student discusses positive and negative consequences of behaviors in problem situations.

**The Best Thing to Do/The Worst Thing to Do**

| Situation: | |
|---|---|
| *Behaviors* | *Consequences* |
| Positive<br>Talk to people in neighborhood where jewelry was found.<br>Put ad in paper.<br>Notify police department.<br>Ask parents what to do. | Jewelry could be returned to owner.<br>Personal satisfaction because of honesty.<br>Possible reward. |
| Negative<br>Keep it.<br>Sell it and keep the money.<br>Leave it where it was.<br>Give it to your mother and tell her you bought it. | May be accused of stealing.<br>Feelings of guilt<br>May get in trouble with parents, school personnel, or police. |

**Domain:** Personal-Social Skills
**Competency:** 15. Achieving Problem-Solving Skills
**Subcompetency:** 67. Understanding the Need for Goals

# Setting Goals for a Class Newspaper

*Academic Components*

Language (Listening)
Language (Oral Expression)

*Objectives*

1. The student will discuss the need for setting goals for a group project.

2. With a group, the student will set goals for a project.

*Types of Activity*

Discussion
Small Group

*Activity*

1. Discuss with the class the importance of setting goals and following through on goals when working on a group project. What would happen if each member of the group were striving for a different goal?
2. Present to the class the idea of working together on a class newspaper. Have the class set goals and record them on the board. Goals should be related to the content, length, and completion date of the newspaper.
3. Divide the class into groups of three or four. Each group is responsible for one or two sections of the newspaper (class/school news, entertainment, sports, food, advice column, social news, etc.).
4. Assist each group in setting a group goal and individual steps to be taken to reach that goal.
5. At the completion of the project, discuss with the class their success in achieving the goals they had set.
   (a) Were the goals realistic?
   (b) Did all members of the group work towards achieving the goals?
   (c) Were there some other goals that should have been set?

*Follow-up; Evaluation*

On a checklist, the teacher notes the amount and level of individual participation in the group goal-setting activity and contribution to group discussion.

**Domain:** Personal-Social Skills
**Competency:** 15. Achieving Problem-Solving Skills
**Subcompetency:** 68. Looking at Alternatives

# There's More than One Way to . . .

*Academic Components*

Language (Oral Expression)
Language (Written Expression)

*Types of Activity*

Discussion
Small Group

*Objective*

The student will be able to list alternative ways to achieve a goal or solve a problem.

*Activity*

1. Introduce this activity by presenting the class with a goal or problem. Ask the students, "What is the *one* way to achieve this goal (or solve this problem)?" Allow open discussion. As the students disagree on the one appropriate response, stop the discussion and suggest that there might be more than one appropriate answer. List all alternatives the students can think of on the board.
2. Students work individually or in small groups. Each student/group is given a goal or problem. The students write as many alternatives to reaching the goal or solving the problem as they can. The teacher and aide assist as needed. Some examples of goals and problems are:
   (a) Improving grade in math class
   (b) Getting a summer job
   (c) Resolving conflicts with siblings
   (d) Need for transportation to the beach
   (e) Having a broken bicycle
3. As a class, discuss the alternatives the student/groups have listed. Discuss the appropriateness of each alternative.

*Follow-up; Evaluation*

Given a goal or a problem the student lists at least three alternate ways to reach the goal or solve the problem.

**Domain:** Personal-Social Skills
**Competency:** 15. Achieving Problem-Solving Skills
**Subcompetency:** 69. Anticipating Consequences

# What Happens if I Don't Do It?

*Academic Components*

Language (Oral Expression)
Language (Written
Expression)

*Types of Activity*

Discussion
Worksheet
Home Involvement

*School/Community Resource
Person*

Parent

*Objective*

The student will be able to list consequences of not following through on responsibilities.

*Activity*

1. Discuss daily responsibilities the students have at home and at school. Discuss consequences of not following through on responsibilities. Are others affected or just the student? (The consequence of forgetting lunch money affects only the student; the consequence of not coming home in time to babysit affects others.)

2. Each student lists daily responsibilities at home and at school. (Parents should help in this.) The student lists consequences of not following through on the responsibilities and who is affected (see example).

*Follow-up; Evaluation*

1. The student lists at least five daily responsibilities and the consequences for not doing them.
2. As a follow-up activity, the students can keep weekly records of responsibilities, checking when they did or did not follow through on them, and making a note of the positive or negative consequences.

**What Happens If I Don't Do It?**

| Responsibility | Consequence | Who is Affected? |
|---|---|---|
| 1. Get to school on time. | Detention | me |
| 2. Do homework | Lower grades | me; parents upset |
| 3. Take out trash | Loss of allowance, smelly kitchen | Family |
| 4. Feed dogs | Dogs go hungry | Dogs |

**Domain:** Personal-Social Skills
**Competency:** 15. Achieving Problem-Solving Skills
**Subcompetency:** 70. Knowing Where to Find Good Advice

# Who Can Help Me?

*Academic Component*

Language (Oral Expression)

*Types of Activity*

Discussion
Small Group

*Objective*

The student will list resources for seeking advice for a variety of situations.

*Activity*

1. Discuss the importance of recognizing when advice is needed and knowing where to find good advice. Emphasize that no one has all of the answers all of the time, and help from different sources may be needed to solve different problems.
2. Develop a class list of resources for seeking advice. Some resources that may be included are:
   parents
   teachers
   friends
   medical services
   legal services
   counselor
   clergy
   prayer
   community agencies
   psychological services
3. Present the class with several situations in which a teenager needs to seek advice. Individually or in a group, the students list the resources (from the list developed by the class) appropriate for each situation. Some examples of situations are:
   (a) academic failure
   (b) girlfriend/boyfriend problems
   (c) overweight
   (d) pregnancy
   (e) depression
   (f) health problems
   (g) drug/alcohol abuse

*Follow-up; Evaluation*

Given a problem situation in which a teenager is in need of advice, the student lists at least two appropriate resources for seeking advice.

**Domain:** Personal-Social Skills
**Competency:** 16. Communicating Adequately with Others
**Subcompetency:** 71. Recognizing Emergency Situations

# Help!

*Academic Components*

Language (Oral and
   Written Expression)

*Objective*

The student will be able to list appropriate behaviors in emergency situations.

*Activity*

1. Discuss emergency situations and the responsibilities of people involved in

*Types of Activity*

Discussion
Small Group
Role Play

giving or seeking assistance.

2. Students work in pairs. Each pair is given a situation involving an emergency. The students write a skit to demonstrate appropriate behavior in giving or seeking assistance.

Example: Maria and Andy are walking home from school.
Maria: Do you smell smoke?
Andy: Yes! Look! That house is on fire!
Maria: Oh, no! There are children in there!
Andy:
Maria:
Andy:
Maria: (Students complete the skit.)

Example: Joe and Fred are working on an assembly line. A coworker's shirt sleeve gets caught in a machine.
Joe:
Fred: (Students complete the skit.)

3. Each group reads its skit to the class. The class discusses the appropriateness of the responses and offers other suggestions.

*Follow-up; Evaluation*

Given an emergency situation, the student lists at least two ways to give or seek assistance.

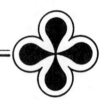

**Domain:** Personal-Social Skills
**Competency:** 16. Communicating Adequately with Others
**Subcompetency:** 72. Reading at Level Needed for Future Goals

## Getting the Newspaper Habit

*Academic Components*

Reading
Language (Oral Expression)

*Objective*

The student will read and report on one newspaper article daily.

with each section. Include: National/World News, Local News, Sports, Entertainment, Weather, Classified Ads, Editorial Pages, Food, etc.

*Types of Activity*

Discussion
Bulletin Board

*Activity*

1. Show the students the different sections of the newspaper and the type of information contained in each.
2. Arrange to have a newspaper in class daily. (Have a paper delivered to the school, bring your own, or ask parents to volunteer for a week at a time.)
3. Each week, assign each student a section of the newspaper to read. Set aside time each day for newspaper reading. Choose a few students to report on what they read that day. Rotate sections each week so the students become familiar

*Follow-up; Evaluation*

1. The student reads at least one newspaper article daily and briefly discusses it.
2. A bulletin board can be made of the most interesting articles each week.

*Note*: Objectives for meeting this subcompetency should be included throughout the student's entire curriculum. Provide activities involving reading the telephone directory, signs and labels, owner's manuals, recipes, state driver's handbook, menus, travel brochures, etc.

**Domain:** Personal-Social Skills
**Competency:** 16. Communicating Adequately with Others
**Subcompetency:** 73. Writing at the Level Needed for Future Goals

# Get the Message

*Academic Components*

Language (Listening)
Language (Oral Expression)
Language (Written
  Expression)

*Types of Activity*

Discussion
Demonstration

*Objective*

The student will be able to take an accurate telephone message.

*Activity*

1. Discuss situations in which it is important to take accurate telephone messages (parents are out, babysitting, on the job, etc.)
2. Demonstrate and discuss good note-taking techniques:
    (a) Jot down brief notes first, then write out complete message after hanging up.
    (b) Ask caller to please spell name, if necessary.
    (c) Repeat numbers and dates back to the caller to verify accuracy.
    (d) Be polite.
    (e) Never try to take a message without a pencil and paper handy.

(f) Students with limited writing ability should write only the caller's name and telephone number. Politely ask the caller to spell and repeat when needed.
3. Pre-record telephone conversations from which messages need to be taken. Include only the caller's voice on the tape. Provide the student with a telephone message pad. The student listens to the tape and writes the message on the pad.

*Follow-up; Evaluation*

1. The teacher (or aide) listens to the tape with the student to verify the accuracy of the written message. Offer suggestions when necessary.
2. This activity and Subcompetency 74 ("Can You Understand Me?") can be included in a Communications Learning Center.

**Domain:** Personal-Social Skills
**Competency:** 16. Communicating Adequately with Others
**Subcompetency:** 74. Speaking Adequately for Understanding

# Can You Understand Me?

*Academic Components*

Language (Oral Expression)
Language (Listening)
Reading

*Objective*

The student will improve oral communication in a variety of situations.

*Activity*

1. Provide the student with a variety of opportunities to record and evaluate speaking ability.

*Types of Activity*

Role Play
Demonstration
Worksheet

(a) Student reads a newspaper article or section from a book into the tape recorder.
(b) Pre-record questions; student records answers on the tape.
(c) Role play conversations; student records responses on the tape (conversations between friends, with a best friend's mother, storekeeper, etc.).
(d) Pre-record employment interview; student records responses on the tape.
(e) Student records telephone conversations in which he or she is seeking information (what hours the library is open, does a store carry a certain product, etc.).

2. After completing one of the above activities, the student listens to the tape again and fills out an evaluation form (see example).

1. After listening to the tape, the teacher discusses the evaluation form with the student and offers suggestions for improvement.
2. This activity can be done weekly; note improvement on evaluation forms.
3. This activity and Subcompetency 73 ("Get the Message!") can be included in a Communications Learning Center.

## Can You Understand Me?

| *Self-Evaluation—Speaking* | |
| --- | --- |
| 1. Was my voice | too loud? <br> too soft? <br> just right? |
| 2. Did I speak | too fast? <br> too slowly? <br> just right? |
| 3. Were my sentences | complete? <br> incomplete? <br> one-word answers only? |
| 4. Did I answer questions | correctly? <br> incorrectly? |
| 5. Did I use words and phrases | appropriate to the situation? <br> inappropriate to the situation? |
| 6. Overall, was my speaking | easy to understand? <br> difficult to understand? |
| *Teacher comments/suggestions:* | |

**Domain:** Personal-Social Skills
**Competency:** 16. Communicating Adequately with Others
**Subcompetency:** 75. Understanding the Subtleties of Communication

# It's Not Always What You Say, but How You Say It

*Academic Components*

Language (Oral Expression)
Visual Perception

*Types of Activity*

Discussion
Role Play

*Objective*

The student will be able to identify and demonstrate verbal and nonverbal means of communication.

*Activity*

1. Introduce this activity by showing the class several photographs depicting different facial expressions and gestures. Have the students write (or tell orally) a caption for each picture, telling what the person might be saying.
2. Discuss the subtleties of communication: tone of voice, rate of speech, facial expressions, body language, gestures, etc. Demonstrate how the same sentence can have different meanings, depending on how it is spoken.
3. If a video camera is available, film actors in short skits portraying a variety of emotions and situations. (Enlist the aid of the drama class or a group of teachers to serve as actors.) Play each skit for the class, with the sound turned off. The students discuss their perceptions of the situation in the skit. Replay the skit with the sound on; students discuss the accuracy of their responses.

   (If video camera equipment is not available, have the students watch a television program with the sound turned off. They discuss what they think is happening in the program.)
4. On another day, have the students listen to tape recorded conversations. Play the tape a second time; students show expressions and gestures to go along with the conversations.

*Follow-up; Evaluation*

1. Given a picture or video recording showing facial expressions and gestures, the student gives a statement (orally or written) that is consistent with the visual presentation.
2. Given a taped recording of conversation, the student demonstrates facial expressions and gestures consistent with the conversation.

# 3. Occupational Skills

## Competencies

17. Knowing and Exploring Occupational Possibilities
18. Selecting and Planning Occupational Choices
19. Exhibiting Appropriate Work Habits and Behaviors
20. Exhibiting Sufficient Physical-Manual Skills
21. Obtaining a Specific Occupational Skill
22. Seeking, Securing, and Maintaining Employment

**Domain:** Occupational Skills
**Competency:** 17. Knowing and Exploring Occupational Possibilities
**Subcompetency:** 76. Identifying the Personal Values Met Through Work

## Why Work?

*Academic Components*

Language (Oral Expression)
Reading

*Types of Activity*

Discussion
Worksheet

*Objective*

The student will compare personal values met through work and school.

*Activity*

1. Give the student a worksheet to complete, telling the reasons for going to school (see example). The student responds "yes," "no," or "don't know" to the statements in Column A (labeled ("School").
2. Discuss the worksheets with the entire class. Note similarities and differences among the students' responses.

3. Ask the student if they think they would get a job for the same reasons. Instruct them to label Column B "Job." The students respond to the same set of statements, this time giving reasons why they would get a job.
4. In a class discussion, compare the similarities and differences between Column A and Column B.

*Follow-up; Evaluation*

1. The student identifies personal values met through school.
2. The student compares personal values met by going to school and work by completing worksheet.

### Why Work?

Why do you go to school? Answer each statement with "yes," "no," or "don't know" in Column A. Wait for instructions from your teacher before you write anything in Column B.

|  | Column A *(School)* | Column B *(        )* |
|---|---|---|
| 1. It's a law. | | |
| 2. My parents make me. | | |
| 3. I get paid for it. | | |
| 4. I need to learn a lot of things. | | |
| 5. It's a place to see my friends. | | |
| 6. I want to improve myself. | | |
| 7. I feel secure. | | |
| 8. I feel good when I do well. | | |
| 9. Other people depend on me to do a good job. | | |
| 10. I can meet new friends. | | |
| 11. I have a chance to be involved in many activities. | | |
| 12. I would get punished if I didn't. | | |
| Write your own reasons not listed above: | | |

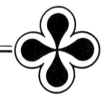

**Domain:** Occupational Skills
**Competency:** 17. Knowing and Exploring Occupational Possibilities
**Subcompetency:** 77. Identify the Societal Values Met through Work

## Let's All Work Together

*Academic Components*

Language (Oral Expression)
Language (Listening)

*Types of Activity*

Discussion
Small Group

*Objective*

The student will identify ways in which different workers are dependent on each other.

*Activity*

1. Discuss the necessity for having such a wide variety of jobs in our society. Dis-cuss the importance of menial tasks as well as jobs with more prestige. What would happen if no one did certain jobs; how would that affect society?

2. Divide the class into small groups. Each group is given a place of employment: an office, store, restaurant, construction site, etc. The students list all the jobs that might be found at that workplace. How do workers on the different jobs help each other? The students dis-

cuss what would happen if one or more of the workers failed to do his job.
3. Each group briefly reports to the class.

*Follow-up; Evaluation*

Given a place of employment, the student discusses ways in which workers at that workplace are interdependent.

**Domain:** Occupational Skills
**Competency:** 17. Knowing and Exploring Occupational Possibilities
**Subcompetency:** 78. Identifying the Remunerative Aspects of Work

# Am I Earning Enough?

*Academic Components*

Math
Reading
Language (Oral Expression)
Language (Vocabulary)

*Types of Activity*

Discussion
Worksheet

*Objective*

The student will be able to determine whether or not a worker's net pay is adequate to meet expenses.

*Activity*

1. Discuss with the class the different ways workers are paid: hourly, weekly, monthly, by the job, etc.
2. Discuss basic expenses that must be included in a budget: rent, food, utilities, transportation, clothing, entertainment, etc. Have students identify which expenses are usually monthly, weekly, daily, or other.
3. Show students an example of a paycheck stub and how to locate the net pay. Write a list of monthly expenses on the board. Instruct the students to add the expenses to find the total. De-

termine whether this paycheck is large enough to cover the listed expenses.
4. Students complete a worksheet (see example) with problems similar to the one in #3.
5. Discuss the students's findings:
   (a) Which person(s) have enough money to pay the bills?
   (b) Which persons(s) do not have enough money to pay the bills?
   (c) Are there any expenses not listed?
   (d) What are some things a person can do if the paycheck is not large enough to meet expenses?

*Follow-up; Evaluation*

1. The student correctly answers two of the three problems on the worksheet.
2. The student discusses solutions to the problem of not earning enough money to meet expenses.

**Am I Earning Enough?**

1. RICK   Net pay: $850.00 per month

| | | | |
|---|---|---|---|
| Rent | $325.00 | Insurance | $25.00 |
| Utilities | 52.00 | Clothes | 30.00 |
| Food | 175.00 | Recreation | 30.00 |
| Bus fare | 12.00 | Furniture payment | 32.00 |

Total Expenses: _____
Does Rick have enough money this month? _____

2. JENNY   Net pay: $275 per week

| | | | |
|---|---|---|---|
| Rent | $475.00 | Car payment | $75.00 |
| Utilities | 60.00 | Recreation | 50.00 |
| Food | 250.00 | Car Ins. | 80.00 |
| Gas | 30.00 | Savings | 25.00 |
| Clothes | 50.00 | Gifts | 30.00 |

Total Expenses: _____
Does Jenny have enough money this month? _____

3. CHARLES   Gross pay: $5.50 per hour; 40 hours per week

| | | | |
|---|---|---|---|
| Deductions: | $150.00 | Subway fare | $18.00 |
| Rent: | 280.00 | Recreation | 15.00 |
| Food | 200.00 | Savings | 10.00 |
| Utilities | 36.00 | Clothes | 25.00 |
| Church | 50.00 | Bicycle repair | 30.00 |

Total Expenses: _____
Does Charles have enough money this month?

**Domain:** Occupational Skills
**Competency:** 17. Knowing and Exploring Occupational Possibilities
**Subcompetency:** 79. Understanding Classification of Jobs into Different
Occupational Systems

# It's in the Cards

*Academic Components*

Social Studies
Reading

*Type of Activity*

Game

*Objective*

The student will become aware of the classification of jobs into occupational clusters.

*Activity*

1. This activity requires the preparation of a deck of cards. This may be time-consuming for the teacher and/or aide, but the cards can be used for several activities. Using 10 to 15 career clusters (Construction, Manufacturing, Transportation, Agri-Business/Natural Resources, Marine Science, Environmental, Business and Office, Marketing and Distribution, Communications and Media, Hospitality and Recreation, Personal Service, Public Service, Health, Consumer and Home-making, Fine Arts and Humanities),

make four job cards for each category. Number the job cards 1 through 4 according to the level of the job: Lower numbers indicate the least training and experience; higher numbers indicate the most training and experience (see examples). Pictures may or may not be used on the card. Laminate the cards before using.

2. Discuss occupational clusters and how jobs are placed in these clusters. Discuss the wide variety of jobs within each cluster.

3. Games:
   (a) "Careers Rummy" 2–4 players
      1. Deal 7 cards to each player.
      2. In turn, each player draws a card and discards. (Players may draw from the discard pile.)
      3. When a player has all four cards in one category, he or she lays them down on the table.
      4. The first player to lay down all cards wins.
   (b) Variation—Players can lay down two-card sets. The object is to have the highest number of points laid down when all cards have been played.
   (c) As a group activity, the teacher holds the deck of cards and draws one card at a time. The students take turns giving another job in the category of the job card drawn. (Jobs may not be repeated!)
   (d) Use your imagination!

*Follow-up; Evaluation*

Given a career cluster, the student identifies at least three jobs within the cluster.

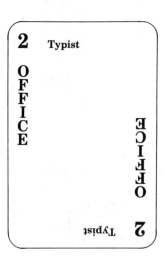

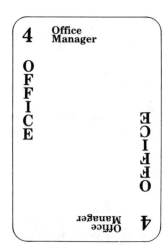

**Domain:** Occupational Skills
**Competency:** 17. Knowing and Exploring Occupational Possibilities
**Subcompetency:** 80. Identifying Occupational Opportunities Available Locally

## Finding Available Jobs

*Academic Components*

Reading
Language (Oral Expression)
Language (Written
  Expression)

*Types of Activity*

Research
Small Group
Discussion

*Objective*

The student will be able to locate local jobs available by using the classified section of the newspaper.

*Activity*

1. Show the students how to locate the classified section of the newspaper listing available occupational opportunities. Show how the jobs are listed alphabetically or by general category.
2. Students work individually or in pairs. Each student or pair is given one or more pages of the classified section listing jobs. The students make a list of all the jobs listed on that page (or pages), and the number of times each job is listed.
3. Students report their findings to the class. List the jobs with the highest number of entries on the board. Discuss these jobs in relation to the students' interest, abilities, training, and experience.

*Follow-up; Evaluation*

1. Using the classified section of the newspaper, the student demonstrates how to locate available jobs.
2. The student can research one of the high-frequency jobs.

**Domain:** Occupational Skills
**Competency:** 17. Knowing and Exploring Occupational Possibilities
**Subcompetency:** 81. Identifying Sources of Occupational Information

## Sources of Information about Jobs

*Academic Components*

Social Studies
Reading

*Objective*

The student will be able to identify sources of occupational information and the kinds of information available from each source.

*Activity*

1. Discuss with the students different sources for investigating occupations: *Occupational Outlook Handbook, Dictionary of Occupational Titles,* news-

*Types of Activity*

Research
Guest Speaker

*School/Community Resource Persons*

Employment Agency
   Personnel
Business or Industry
   Representative

paper, school counselor, employment offices, brochures from business and industry, etc.

2. Invite a representative from an employment office, business, or industry to discuss with the class how to obtain information on jobs, and what kind of information they provide.

3. Compile materials listed in #1; place on bulletin board and/or Careers Center in the classroom. Students can use this center to locate information on specific jobs of interest. It can also be used with other activities in the Occupational Skills Domain.

*Follow-up; Evaluation*

1. The student can list at least three sources of occupational information.

2. For each source listed, the student is able to tell at least one type of information provided.

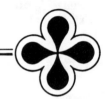

**Domain:** Occupational Skills
**Competency:** 18. Selecting and Planning Occupational Choices
**Subcompetency:** 82. Identifying Major Occupational Needs

# What Do I Need in a Job?

*Academic Components*

Language (Oral Expression)
Language (Written
   Expression)
Reading

*Types of Activity*

Discussion
Worksheet

*Objective*

The student will become aware of personal needs in making occupational choices.

*Activity*

1. Discuss the differences in occupational needs among individuals. Stress that different people choose different occupations because of different needs, interests, and abilities.

2. Instruct the students to write the titles of three jobs they think they would like to have someday. Save this list.

3. Administer a published job-related interest/needs inventory or prepare one of your own (see example).

4. After completing the inventory, have the students compare their responses to the requirements of the three jobs they chose at the beginning of the activity.

5. Discuss: According to the inventory, would one (or all) of these jobs meet your personal needs?

*Follow-up; Evaluation*

1. The student completes the inventory and discusses responses in relation to occupational choices.

2. This activity may be included in the Careers Notebook (Subcompetency 86.)

**Inventory of Occupational Interests/Needs**
**Sample Questions**

*Directions*: For each question, circle the letter of the statement you would rather do.

I would rather . . .

1. a. work outside.
   b. work inside.

2. a. work alone.
   b. work with a lot of people.

3. a. work at a desk.
   b. work at an active job.

4. a. work in a noisy place.
   b. work in a quiet place.

5. a. have a job that pays a lot of money.
   b. have a job that is fun and personally satisfying.

6. a. work at different tasks all the time.
   b. work at the same task all day.

7. a. work according to a schedule.
   b. set my own schedule.

8. a. work with my hands.
   b. work with people.

9. a. work for a large company.
   b. work for a small business.

10. a. work for myself.
    b. work for someone else.

11. a. supervise other workers.
    b. have someone supervise me.

12. a. work in the daytime.
    b. work at night.

13. a. work in a large city.
    b. work in a small town.

14. a. work with machines.
    b. work with people

15. a. travel with my job.
    b. work in the same town all the time.

**Domain:** Occupational Skills
**Competency:** 18. Selecting and Planning Occupational Choices
**Subcompetency:** 83. Identifying Major Occupational Interests

# Would I Like This Job?

*Academic Components*

Social Studies
Language (Oral Expression)
Language (Written Expression)
Reading

*Types of Activity*

Discussion
Research

*Objective*

The student will list jobs she thinks she would and would not like; the student will be able to list pros and cons of jobs.

*Activity*

1. Discuss the importance of individual differences in job choices. Elicit responses from the students about jobs they think they might like to have some day. Stress that they do not have to make major occupational choices in junior high, but that it is important to begin exploring job possibilities.

2. Students individually make two lists:

(a) *Jobs I Might Like to Have Someday*
(b) *Jobs I Know I Would Never Want to Have*

(At least five responses per list.)

3. Choose one job from each list for each student. The student finds out and lists at least three pros and at least three cons for both of the jobs.

(a) *Areas to research*: Amount and kind of training required, pay, hours, working conditions, opportunity for advancement, availability, special skills required, etc.

(b) *Possible sources of information*: Resource materials in the classroom, library, parents, interviews with neighbors and others in the community, newspaper.

4. The student re-evaluates the two jobs by answering the following questions:
   (a) Do you still think you would like this job?
   (b) Do you still think you would never want this job?

*Follow-up; Evaluation*

The student lists two jobs he thinks he would or would not like and gives two reasons why he would or would not like each job.

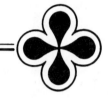

**Domain:** Occupational Skills
**Competency:** 18. Selecting and Planning Occupational Choices
**Subcompetency:** 84. Identifying Occupational Aptitudes

# Can You Do This?

*Academic Components*

Social Studies
Language (Vocabulary)
Language (Oral Expression)
Language (Written Expression)
Reading

*Types of Activity*

Discussion
Worksheet

*Objective*

The student will identify aptitudes required on specific jobs and identify personal aptitudes.

*Activity*

1. Discuss aptitudes and how they relate to job performance. Discuss terms used to describe aptitudes, such as "dexterity" and "perception." Include in your discussion two or three jobs and ask students to list aptitudes necessary for those jobs. Use the *Dictionary of Occupational Titles* to verify aptitudes listed and to identify aptitudes the students did not list.
2. Instruct the students to choose two jobs in which they have an interest. Using the *Dictionary of Occupational Titles* and other materials used for the Careers Notebook (see Subcompetency 89), the student identifies the aptitudes required for each job. The aptitudes can be listed or checked off on a worksheet (see example).
3. Administer a published aptitude test to the students, or use informal teacher-made evaluations of performance. As a result of these tests, the students rate themselves on the aptitudes listed.
4. The students determine whether or not they have the aptitudes necessary for each job, and which aptitudes they can improve.

*Follow-up; Evaluation*

1. The student identifies aptitudes required for at least one job.
2. The student identifies personal aptitudes.
3. The teacher works with individual students in developing a plan to improve aptitudes.
4. This activity can be included in the Careers Notebook (Subcompetency 86).

**Occupational Aptitudes**

1. Check (√) the aptitudes required for each job. Write in others not already listed.
2. When you rate yourself on these aptitudes,
   write + if you do it very well,
   write √ if you do it OK,
   write − if you don't do it well.

| *Aptitudes* | *Job #1* | *Job #2* | *ME* |
|---|---|---|---|
| speed | | | |
| accuracy | | | |
| dexterity | | | |
| eye-hand coordination | | | |
| reading | | | |
| calculation | | | |
| strength | | | |
| coordination | | | |
| form perception | | | |
| spatial relations | | | |
| others: | | | |

3. Do you have the aptitudes for Job #1? _____ Job #2? _____
4. Which aptitudes would you like to improve?

**Domain:** Occupational Skills
**Competency:** 18. Selecting and Planning Occupational Choices
**Subcompetency:** 85. Identifying Requirements of Appropriate and Available Jobs

# A Job for Me

*Academic Components*

Social Studies
Language (Oral Expression)
Language (Written
  Expression)

*Types of Activity*

Discussion
Guest Speaker
Research

*Objective*

The student will be able to identify the requirements of a job that is presently available.

*Activity*

Conduct this activity near the end of the school year, when many students may be looking for summer jobs.

1. In a class discussion, ask students to tell what jobs they have already had. List these jobs on the board. Make another list of jobs the students think they could do this summer (babysitting, gardening, animal care, washing cars, housecleaning, etc.).

2. Invite the school counselor or a representative from a Youth Employment Service to inform the students of available jobs for the summer. (Be sure to include information on work permits that are required for some jobs.) If brochures are not available, develop one with the counselor so students will have it for reference.

3. Each student chooses one or more jobs of interest. Using the available information, and talking to the counselor or Youth Employment Service representative, the student makes a list of requirements for each job: training, experience, skills, etc. The student determines whether or not he or she is qualified for the job.

*School/Community Resource Persons*

School Counselor
Youth Employment Service Representative

*Follow-up; Evaluation*

1. The student identifies the requirement of at least one job available for the summer.

2. Encourage students to apply for jobs when appropriate.
3. Follow up and encourage students who do apply and obtain summer employment.

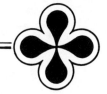

**Domain:** Occupational Skills
**Competency:** 18. Selecting and Planning Occupational Choices
**Subcompetency:** 86. Making Realistic Occupational Choices

# Careers Notebook

*Academic Components*

Social Studies
Reading
Language (Oral Expression)
Language (Written Expression)
Language (Vocabulary)

*Types of Activity*

Discussion
Notebook/Research
Bulletin Board

*Objective*

The student will explore a variety of occupational categories and begin developing occupational preferences.

*Activity*

1. Have the students compile a careers notebook—an activity to be continued throughout the school year. The first unit should be an introduction to careers. Each succeeding unit should introduce a new occupational category.
2. Introductory unit can include:
   (a) The definition of a career.
   (b) Vocabulary used in the world of work.
   (c) Activities to stimulate the students to begin thinking about jobs they would like to have.
   (d) Draw pictures or make a collage of people in different jobs.
3. All other units should include:
   (a) Discussion and opening activity to familiarize the students with the types of jobs in a specific occupational category.
   (b) Vocabulary—job titles and terms used on the job. Activities can include word search and crossword puzzles, dictionary practice, sentence writing, or fill-in-the-blanks. The words can also be used for spelling lessons!
   (c) Exploration of jobs—use published materials, information from employers, guest speakers, field trips,

library research, the newspaper, etc. It is helpful to have a Careers Center and Bulletin Board in the classroom so all materials are readily available.
   (d) Role-play situations involving jobs in this category.
   (e) At least one activity should require the student to begin making decisions about job preferences.
   (f) Extra-credit activities can include creative writing, drawing pictures, collecting further information about the jobs, interviewing workers having the jobs in this category, researching and bringing to class uniforms and/or tools, checking on the availability of these jobs in your community, etc.
4. Provide at least one class period per week for working on the notebook. Students can also work on the notebooks in their free time or at home. Work with the students as a group and individually.

*Follow-up; Evaluation*

1. Set a due date for each unit. Evaluate notebooks periodically to monitor students' progress. Give extra credit for students who complete all assignments in a unit on time.
2. At the completion of each unit, the student names at least one job he or she would most like from the jobs in that category.

**Domain:** Occupational Skills
**Competency:** 19. Exhibiting Appropriate Work Habits and Behaviors
**Subcompetency:** 87. Following Directions

# Ten Ways to Keep Your Job and Not Get Fired

*Academic Components*

Reading
Language (Oral Expression)
(Behavior Management)

*Types of Activity*

Discussion
Chart/Bulletin Board
(Behavior Management)

*Objectives*

1. The student will understand and follow posted classroom rules and guidelines.
2. The student will identify ways in which following directions at school is similar to or different from following directions at work.

*Activity*

1. Post a chart in the classroom listing classroom rules in "job" terminology (see example).
2. At the beginning of the school year, explain to the students how the work habits they develop now will help them when they are older and get a job. Discuss all rules in relation to both the world of work and school. Review the chart several times during the first month of school; thereafter, refer to it as needed.

*Follow-up; Evaluation*

1. The student shows improvement in following classroom rules.

2. Given a classroom rule, the student tells how it is the same or different from rules at work.

**Ten Ways to Keep Your Job
(And Not Get Fired!)**

1. Go to work every day.
2. Be on time.
3. Be prepared.
4. Follow your supervisor's directions.
5. Do your very best work all the time.
6. Finish all your work.
7. Be kind and cooperative with other workers.
8. Respect the rights and property of others.
9. Keep your work area neat.
10. Remember that a friendly worker will always be more successful than an unpleasant worker!

**Domain:** Occupational Skills
**Competency:** 19. Exhibiting Appropriate Work Habits and Behaviors
**Subcompetency:** 88. Working with Others

# Job Ratings

*Academic Components*

Reading
(Behavior Management)

*Types of Activity*

Discussion
(Behavior Management)
Home Involvement

*School/Community Resource
Person*

Parent

*Objective*

The student will show improvement in working with peers and in completing class assignments.

*Activity*

1. Develop a point system in which students receive points daily for categories such as punctuality, bringing materials, completion of assignments, and getting along well with others in the classroom. Ten points can be made possible daily (or per class period) with the

Refer to these points as "Job Ratings" (see example).

3. Construct a chart explaining what the "Job Ratings" mean (see example). Post this chart in the classroom. Discuss individual job ratings weekly.

4. Getting fired—failure to reach a certain number of points during the week results in getting fired.
   (a) First time:
       1. Letter to parents and student (see example)
       2. Rehire conference (see example of memo)
   (b) Second time in one quarter: Parents' attendance required at Rehire Conference.

### How's Your Job Rating?

| Period 3 | Week 1 | Week 2 | Week 3 | Week 4 | Week 5 | Week 6 | Week 7 | Week 8 | Week 9 | Week 10 |
|---|---|---|---|---|---|---|---|---|---|---|
| André | 50 | 47 | 51 | | | | | | | |
| Becky | 48 | 51 | 56 | | | | | | | |
| Charles | 53 | 52 | 56 | | | | | | | |
| Diana | 58 | 59 | 57 | | | | | | | |
| Ed | 42 | 45 | 44 | | | | | | | |
| Frank | 36 | 38 | 40 | | | | | | | |
| Gustavo | 49 | 44 | 47 | | | | | | | |
| Harold | 55 | 53 | 53 | | | | | | | |

opportunity to earn bonus points. These points are recorded daily on each student's folder.

2. Make a Job Ratings chart for the class (or each class period) with all students' names listed. At the end of each week, write the total number of points earned on the chart next to the student's name.

*Follow-up; Evaluation*

1. The student improves job ratings (or maintains a rating of "Excellent" or "Very Good" worker).
2. At Rehire Conferences, discuss with the student and/or parents ways in which improvements can be made.

**Job Ratings**

| | |
|---|---|
| 55 + | *Excellent Worker*—You consistently do a job in a pleasant, cooperative manner. Any boss would be glad to hire you! |
| 50–54 | *Very Good Worker*—You usually try very hard and get the job done. You get along well with others. |
| 45–49 | *Fair Worker*—You usually do well, but you don't really try your hardest. You might be having some problems with other workers. |
| 40–44 | *Poor Worker*—If you don't shape up, you're in danger of getting fired! |
| 39 – | *You're Fired!* No boss wants a worker who does not follow directions, does not get along with others, and does a poor job!<br><br>Rehire Conference (detention) required. Parent conference required if fired more than once per quarter. |

**Letter to Parents and Student**

Date:

To:   (Student's name)
From:   (Teacher's name)

Because of the low points you earned last week, you have been "fired" from __(subject)__. You earned only _(number)_ points out of a possible _____ points. _____ points are required for acceptable work behavior.

Your required "rehire conference" (detention) has been set for ___(date)___ at _(time)_. We will discuss ways in which you can improve behavior to keep you on the job.

Failure to cooperate will result in an office referral, a parent conference, or both.

I will attend the conference (detention) as scheduled.

Student signature: _____

Date: _____

:::::::::::::::::::::::::::::::::::::::::::::::::::::::::::::::::::::::::::::::::::::::::

I understand that _(name of student)_ 's behavior was not acceptable last week. He/she will attend detention as scheduled.

Parent signature: _____

Date: _____

(*Note:* Have the student sign the letter and be responsible for taking it to his parents for their signature. Keep a carbon copy of all letters and memos.)

**Rehire Conference Memo**

Name: _____  Date: _____

Participants:


Reason for conference:

_____ points in _____(subject)_____, week of _____

_____ points in _____, week of _____

_____ points in _____, week of _____

Major problem areas:



Steps to be taken by employee to improve:



Consequences of lack of improvement:



Signatures:  Employee: _____

Supervisor: _____

Other: _____

_____

---

**Domain:** Occupational Skills
**Competency:** 19. Exhibiting Appropriate Work Habits and Behaviors
**Subcompetency:** 89. Working at a Satisfactory Rate

## How Fast Can You Work?

*Academic Components*

Language (Oral Expression)
All Academic Areas


*Types of Activity*

Discussion
Demonstration

*Objective*

The student will work on a school-related task at a satisfactory rate, maintaining accuracy.


*Activity*

1. Discuss reasons why tasks on a job must be performed at a certain rate (pay according to work completed, deadlines to be met, etc.).

2. Discuss reasons why tasks at school must be performed at a certain rate (to earn points for job ratings, grades, learn more, tendency to get in trouble when wasting time, etc.).

3. Choose a school-related task, such as writing spelling words, reading a chapter, or doing math drill. Have the student rate self on expected performance on one or more tasks. For example:

(a) How many spelling words do you think you can write in three minutes?

(b) How many pages do you think you can read (and understand) in five minutes?

(c) How many minutes do you think it will take you to do these 10 math problems?

4. Using a kitchen timer, time the students on one of the tasks. Stress neatness and accuracy!

5. Have the students compare their actual rates with their estimates. Discuss how rates can be improved:

(a) Inattention to disturbances in the classroom.

(b) Stay in seat.

(c) Eliminate unnecessary behaviors (talking, doodling, etc.)

6. Repeat weekly. This is an activity that takes very little time and can be used easily in all curriculum areas. Vary the activity times each week.

*Follow-up; Evaluation*

The student improves rate of completing a school-related task.

**Domain:** Occupational Skills
**Competency:** 19. Exhibiting Appropriate Work Habits and Behaviors
**Subcompetency:** 90. Accepting Supervision

# You're the Boss

*Academic Components*

Language (Listening)
Language (Oral Expression)

*Types of Activity*

Discussion
Small Group
Worksheet

*Objective*

The student will be able to give and accept supervision in a classroom small-group situation.

*Activity*

1. Discuss the roles of a supervisor and worker in a work situation.

2. Divide the class into groups of three to five students each. Choose one student in each group to act as the supervisor. Give each supervisor a card explaining a game or simple task. It is the supervisor's job to instruct the workers in his or her group and oversee their performance.

3. Each worker completes a Rating Sheet (see example).

4. Repeat until all students have had the opportunity to be supervisor. (This can be done on successive days.)

5. Discuss how the students felt in each of the roles. How could the supervisors improve? How could the workers improve in their cooperation?

*Follow-up; Evaluation*

The student identifies and demonstrates the roles of supervisor and worker in a classroom and/or job-related situation.

**Supervisor Rating Chart**

Name of Supervisor: _____

Name of Worker: _____

Activity: _____

Circle the answer you choose for each question:

1. Did you understand the supervisor's directions?     YES     NO

2. Did the supervisor answer the workers' questions about the directions?
   YES     NO

3. Did you cooperate with the supervisor?     YES     NO

4. Was the supervisor fair in handling problems?     YES     NO

5. Was the supervisor available to help with problems or things you did not understand?     YES     NO

6. How would you rate this supervisor?     GOOD     OKAY     POOR

7. How would you rate your cooperation with this supervisor?
   GOOD     OKAY     POOR

**Domain:** Occupational Skills
**Competency:** 19. Exhibiting Appropriate Work Habits and Behaviors
**Subcompetency:** 91. Recognizing the Importance of Attendance and Punctuality

# What's Your Excuse?

*Academic Components*

Language (Oral Expression)
Language (Listening)

*Types of Activity*

Discussion
Role Play

*Objectives*

1. The student will identify reasons for punctuality and good attendance on the job.
2. The student will differentiate between legitimate and illegitimate excuses for being late or absent.

*Activity*

1. Discuss the reasons why attendance and punctuality are important on the job. (Relate this to "Ten Ways to Keep Your Job and Not Get Fired"—Subcompetency 87.)

2. Discuss reasons why workers are late or absent from school and/or work. Differentiate between legitimate and illegitimate reasons.

3. Role play situations involving tardiness or absenteeism:
   (a) Have situations printed on cards (see examples).
   (b) Two students role-play each situation; one is the worker, the other is the supervisor.
   (c) The worker calls (or talks to) the supervisor, giving reason for being late or absent.
   (d) The supervisor determines whether the reason is legitimate or not and responds appropriately.

**What's Your Excuse?**

*Sample Role-Play Situations*

1. Worker is late:
   Car broke down on way to work.
2. Worker is late:
   Went to rock concert last night and got home at 2:00 a.m.
3. Worker is late:
   Missed the bus.
4. Worker is late:
   Grandmother called when ready to leave.
5. Worker is late:
   Alarm didn't go off.
6. Worker is absent:
   Sick with the flu.
7. Worker is absent:
   Out-of-town relatives visiting.
8. Worker is absent:
   Sister was in accident.
9. Worker is absent:
   Nice day to go to the beach.
10. Worker is absent:
    Applying for another job.

*Follow-up; Evaluation*

1. The student lists at least three reasons why punctuality and attendance are important.
2. Given an excuse for tardiness or absenteeism, the student identifies whether it is legitimate or not.
3. The student can monitor his or her own school attendance and punctuality.

**Domain:** Occupational Skills
**Competency:** 19. Exhibiting Appropriate Work Habits and Behaviors
**Subcompetency:** 92. Meeting Demands for Quality Work

# Strive for High Quality

*Academic Components*

Language (Oral Expression)
Reading

*Type of Activity*

Discussion

*Objectives*

1. The student will identify reasons for quality standards on the job and at school.
2. The student will improve quality of classwork.

*Activity*

1. Discuss the importance of quality standards on the job.
   (a) The product or service must meet minimum standards to give the consumer what he or she is paying for.
   (b) Safety—a malfunctioning product may be unsafe.
   (c) Competition—a better product by another company will sell better.
2. Discuss the importance of quality standards and rewards for schoolwork.
   (a) Satisfaction of a job well done.
   (b) Higher grades.
   (c) Better learning.
   (d) Pleasing parents and teachers.
   (e) Developing the habit of producing

**Job Quality Statements**

> Meets minimum standards for this job.
>
> Exceeds minimum standards for this job.
>
> Far below minimum standards for this job. See your supervisor for assistance.
>
> Incomplete—unacceptable.
>
> Completed before deadline. Bonus!
>
> A high quality job. You are an asset to this company!
>
> Extra training required to meet minimum standards for this job.
>
> Poor quality. Put forth more effort next time.
>
> You are to be commended for your effort and quality work.

(A "date received" stamp can also be used as students' papers are turned in.)

quality work in school will aid the student when employed. Emphasize this point.

3. As teachers, we know how important it is to give the students feedback on their work. Comments on students' papers (or oral comments) can be given in job terms (see examples). The comments can be typed ahead of time on address labels and used as stickers to attach to the students' classwork. Have rubber stamps made for frequently used comments. Comments such as these may be more meaningful than just a letter or number grade.

*Follow-up; Evaluation*

1. The student gives (orally or written) at least two reasons for quality work on the job, and at least two reasons for quality work at school.
2. The student shows improvement in the quality of classwork.

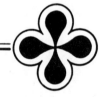

**Domain:** Occupational Skills
**Competency:** 19. Exhibiting Appropriate Work Habits and Behaviors
**Subcompetency:** 93. Demonstrating Occupational Safety

# Is It Safe?

*Academic Components*

Language (Oral Expression)
Social Studies
Reading

*Types of Activity*

Worksheet
Discussion

*Objective*

The student will identify potential hazards and safety precautions to be taken in specific occupations.

*Activity*

1. Discuss common safety hazards at home and at school. Discuss precautions taken to avoid accidents.
2. Relate these safety hazards and precautions to various occupations. Which hazards/precautions are similar? Which are different?

3. As the students investigate occupations, have them fill out a "Job Safety Checklist" for each job explored (see example).

*Follow-up; Evaluation*

1. The student lists at least three potential safety hazards on the job and precautions to be taken to avoid an accident.
2. The "Job Safety Checklist" can be included in the Careers Notebook (Subcompetency 86).
3. Students can observe and make notes of safety hazards/precautions they observe in the community.

**Job Safety Checklist**

Name of Job _____

Description of Job _____

Check all potential safety hazards related to this job:

| | |
|---|---|
| Machinery | Heavy equipment |
| Tools | Excessive noise |
| Chemicals | Excessive cold |
| Fire or excessive heat | Use of ladders/scaffolds |
| Glass | Other: |
| Slippery floors | |

Check safety precautions to be taken on this job:

Special clothing/shoes required
Special gloves required
Goggles or mask required
Special hat required
Ear plugs/protectors required
Special stamina/health requirements
Other:

---

**Domain:** Occupational Skills
**Competency:** 20. Exhibiting Sufficient Physical-Manual Skills
**Subcompetency:** 94. Demonstrating Satisfactory Balance and Coordination

---

# Balance Those Trays!

*Academic Components*

Social Studies
Language (Oral Expression)

*Types of Activity*

Demonstration
Discussion

*Objectives*

1. The student will identify ways in which good balance and coordination are necessary for certain jobs.
2. The student will demonstrate balance and coordination in a work-related activity.

*Activity*

1. Discuss several jobs that require good balance and coordination (construction jobs, waiter/waitress, painter, fireman, etc.). Discuss the ways in which balance and coordination relate to good job performance. Identify jobs in which balance and coordination are not as crucial (desk jobs, some mechanical and factory jobs, teacher, computer operator, etc.). (Note: Fine motor coordination is covered in Subcompetency 95.)

2. Choose a job that requires good balance and coordination, such as a waiter/waitress, for students to demonstrate.
   (a) Provide a large serving tray, like the ones used in restaurants. Also provide plastic or paper dishes: plates, cups, bowls.
   (b) The students take turns balancing dishes on the tray, carrying the tray around the classroom, avoiding obstacles, and serving the dishes to "customers" seated at a table. Have the students first carry the tray with both hands, then with only one hand.
   (c) As the students progress, increase the number of dishes on the tray

and the number of obstacles that must be avoided.

*Follow-up; Evaluation*

1. The student identifies at least three jobs that require good balance and coordination.

2. The student demonstrates satisfactory balance and coordination in a job-related activity.

3. The teacher should work with the P.E. teacher, adaptive P.E. teacher, and/or the parents in developing ways to improve balance and coordination in physically handicapped students.

**Domain:** Occupational Skills
**Competency:** 20. Exhibiting Sufficient Physical-Manual Skills
**Subcompetency:** 95. Demonstrating Satisfactory Manual Dexterity

# Let Your Fingers Do the Working

*Academic Components*

Language (Vocabulary)
Reading
Math

*Types of Activity*

Discussion
Demonstration

*Objective*

The student will be able to perform job-related skills demonstrating satisfactory manual dexterity.

*Activity*

1. Define manual dexterity and discuss jobs in which good manual dexterity is important: Machinist, typist, artist, cabinetmaker, accountant, seamstress, etc.
2. Provide two centers in the classroom: Clerical and Machines/Tools. In each center, have several job-related tasks requiring manual dexterity. The students choose the center they prefer and work on the assigned tasks. After completing the tasks in one center, students may have the option of working in the other center.

    (a) Clerical Center tasks:
    1. Sorting coins into cash register
    2. Using calculator, adding machine, computer and/or typewriter
    3. Filing 3″ × 5″ cards in file box
    4. Copying lists of numbers or names into ledger book

    (b) Machine/Tool Center tasks:
    1. Sorting different sizes of nails and screws
    2. Using screwdriver and wrench to tighten screws, nuts, and bolts
    3. Hammering nails
    4. Cleaning small motors (such as sewing machine motor or electric razor)
    5. Performing operations with simple machines
3. List the tasks for each center on cards. The students rate themselves on performance of the tasks: very good (+), okay (√), poor or difficult (−). Observe the students and discuss areas requiring improvement.
4. Repeat tasks periodically.

*Follow-up; Evaluation*

1. The student demonstrates manual dexterity on three or more job-related tasks. The student shows improvement when necessary.
2. Confer with the parents of students with physical handicaps affecting manual dexterity. Together work out a plan to help the student improve dexterity when applicable.

**Domain:** Occupational Skills
**Competency:** 20. Physical-Manual Skills
**Subcompetency:** 96. Demonstrating Satisfactory Stamina and Endurance

# How Long Can You Work?

*Academic Components*

Language (Vocabulary)
Language (Oral Expression)
Physical Education
Math
Reading

*Types of Activity*

Discussion
Demonstration

*Objective*

The student will be able to perform job-related skills demonstrating satisfactory stamina and endurance.

*Activity*

1. Define "stamina" and "endurance." Discuss jobs in which stamina and endurance are important (construction worker, truck driver, assembly line and other factory workers, typist, etc.). Discuss how some jobs require standing or sitting for long periods of time, or doing the same task over and over.
2. Simulate job skills requiring stamina and endurance. Some examples are:
   (a) Students work math problems all class period while standing at the chalkboard.
   (b) Obtain collating, stapling, and/or envelope-stuffing tasks from the office for the students to work on while standing.
   (c) Provide an "office" in the classroom by using dividers. The student sits at a desk and uses a computer, calculator, or adding machine to add lists of numbers for a specified period of time.
   (d) The student alphabetizes and files a stack of papers while standing.
   (e) Students stack and restack boxes in different parts of the classroom.
3. When students demonstrate proficiency, the amount of time spent on the task can be increased.

*Follow-up; Evaluation*

The student shows increasing proficiency in stamina and endurance while working on job-related tasks.

**Domain:** Occupational Skills
**Competency:** 20. Physical-Manual Skills
**Subcompetency:** 97. Demonstrating Satisfactory Sensory Discrimination

# What Size? What Shape? What Color?

*Academic Components*

Language (Listening)
Visual Perception

*Objective*

The student will satisfactorily perform simple tasks demonstrating size, shape, and color.

*Activity*

1. Discuss jobs in which sensory discrimination is important. Include size, shape, and color.

*Types of Activity*

Demonstration
Discussion

2. Develop classroom activities in which sensory discrimination can be evaluated and practiced:
   (a) Place several common items in a bag or box. Without looking, the student feels each object and describes or identifies it.
   (b) Blindfold students. Have them perform simple tasks (screwing lid on jar, sharpening a pencil, sorting objects by size or shape, etc.).
   (c) Obtain paint chips from a hardware store. The students sort the chips according to color, or arrange the chips of one color in a sequence of light to dark.

*Follow-up; Evaluation*

1. Given a sensory discrimination task, the student will demonstrate satisfactory discrimination.
2. Work individually with students who need improvement in this area.

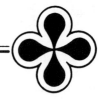

**Domain:** Occupational Skills
**Competency:** 22. Seeking, Securing, and Maintaining Employment
**Subcompetency:** 98. Searching for a Job

# Where Is the Right Job for Me?

*Academic Components*

Language (Oral Expression)
Language (Written Expression)
Language (Listening)

*Types of Activity*

Discussion
Role Play
Worksheet

*Objective*

The student will identify and demonstrate the steps involved in searching for a job.

*Activity*

1. With the class, make a list on the board of resources for finding out about available jobs. Some examples are:
   newspaper
   school counselor
   Youth Employment Service
   State Employment Service
   references from friends
   help wanted signs
2. Through class discussion, develop a list of steps to be taken when searching for a job:
   (a) Check one or more of the resources listed above. List one or more jobs you are interested in.
   (b) Write down information available to you from the resource. Make a list of other information you want to know about the job (or jobs).
   (c) Determine whether you should telephone for an interview or apply in person.
3. Have the students role play calling and asking for an interview.
4. Role play applying for a job in person.
5. Students can use a checklist (see example) of steps to take when searching for a job.

*Follow-up; Evaluation*

1. The student lists and demonstrates by role-play the steps taken in searching for a job.
2. Students may actually call to inquire about jobs after they have practiced by role-play.
3. Follow-up on students who are actually searching for and applying for a job. Give assistance where needed.

**Job Search Checklist**

Source of information about job: _____

Kind of work: _____

Some information you may want to know about the job:
  (If information is not available, ask when you call.)

Location _____

Public transportation available _____

Name of contact person _____

Part-time or full-time? _____

Hours/days of work _____

Experience or training required _____

Is training provided? _____

When can I come in to apply/interview? _____

Amount of pay _____

Health insurance _____

Other Information: _____

_____

Date of initial phone call _____     Time: _____

I talked to _____

Application submitted on (date) _____

Interview:     Date _____

              Time _____

              Place _____

              With _____

**Domain:** Occupational Skills
**Competency:** 22. Seeking, Securing, and Maintaining Employment
**Subcompetency:** 99. Applying for a Job

# Applying for a Job

*Academic Components*

Language (Vocabulary)
Language (Written Expression)
Reading

*Types of Activity*

Discussion
Worksheet

*Objective*

The student will be able to accurately fill out a job application.

*Activity*

1. Discuss terms used in applications for employment. Use these words and phrases for spelling or vocabulary activities. Some examples are:

(a) residence
(b) previous
(c) present
(d) employer
(e) Social Security
(f) print
(g) experience
(h) aptitudes
(i) skills
(j) emergency
(k) verify
(l) signature

**Personal Data Form**

```
 1. Name _____
              Last            First           Middle
 2. Address _____
            Number          Street            Apt.
          _____
            City            State             Zip
 3. Telephone  (    ) _____
 4. In case of emergency notify: _____
    _____
 5. Social Security number _____
 6. Mother's maiden name _____
 7. Date and place of birth _____
                            mo/day/yr      City/State/Country
 8. U.S. citizen?    Yes ___    No ___
 9. Names of schools and dates:
    _____
    _____
    _____
10. Previous employers:
    _____
      Name            Address            Dates
    _____
11. References:
    _____
      Name            Address            Relationship
    _____
    _____
```

(m) references
(n) maiden name

2. Prepare a personal data form for each student (see example). The students fill in the forms with personal information. As a homework assignment, students find out information they don't already know. (Students may not know their zip code, place of birth, or mother's maiden name, for example.) These personal data forms should be neatly filled out and saved for reference when the students actually apply for a job.

3. Collect actual application forms from a variety of businesses. Have the students compare the forms: Do they ask the same or different questions? Is the terminology the same or different? The students practice completing these forms, using their personal data sheet for reference.

*Follow-up; Evaluation*

1. The student correctly and neatly completes an application for employment.
2. Completed application forms can be included in the "Careers Notebook" (Subcompetency 86).
3. Correctly and neatly completed forms can be displayed on a bulletin board.
4. Instruct students on writing personal data in a resume.

---

**Domain:** Occupational Skills
**Competency:** 22. Seeking, Securing, and Maintaining Employment
**Subcompetency:** 100. Interview for a Job

# Job Language

*Academic Components*

Reading
Language (Oral Expression)
Language (Listening)

*Objective*

The student will demonstrate appropriate language when interviewing for a job.

*Activity*

1. Discuss appropriate dress, behavior, and language for a job interview.

2. Give several examples of inappropriate language and how to change to "job language."
Example: Change "Hi, how are ya?" to "Hello, how are you?"

3. Give the students a worksheet listing several statements from an interview (see example). The students choose the statements that demonstrate "job language." The students rewrite inappro-

*Types of Activity*

Discussion
Role Play
Worksheet

priate statements in "job language" (can be done orally).

4. Have the students practice making oral statements in "job language," which may be unfamiliar to many of them.

**"Job Language"**

Circle the number of each statement that shows "job language." On another piece of paper, rewrite the other statements so they show "job language."

1. No, I don't have no experience doin' that there job.
2. I will graduate from high school in June.
3. Yes, I can type 45 words per minute.
4. How much do you guys pay for this job?
5. Yeah, sure.
6. Well, you know, I can, you know, work a machine like, you know, that one over there, you know.
7. I will have to check with my parents, but I think I can start work next Monday.
8. No, I haven't never tooken woodshop at school.
9. I'm sorry, but I will not be able to work nights.
10. No way! You won't catch me doing that kind of work!

5. Role play and tape record mock employment interviews. The teacher or aide is the interviewer; students take turns being interviewed.

6. Replay tapes. The students evaluate themselves on how well they used "job language."

*Follow-up; Evaluation*

1. Given a statement, the student determines whether the language is appropriate for a job interview or not.
2. The student demonstrates the use of appropriate language in a mock job interview.

**Domain:** Occupational Skills
**Competency:** 22. Seeking, Securing, and Maintaining Employment
**Subcompetency:** 101. Adjusting to Competitive Standards

# Improve for Success

*Academic Components*

Language (Oral Expression)
All Academic Areas

*Types of Activity*

Discussion
Personal Consultation

*Objective*

The student will adjust to competitive standards at school.

*Activity*

1. In a class discussion, relate the role of a student to the role of an employee on a job. Discuss the need to make improvements when the quality of work is not up to expectations.
2. Individually counsel the student who is experiencing failure or near-failure in

a regular or special education class.

(a) List and discuss the problems contributing to the student's lack of success (lack of effort, poor attendance, subject matter too difficult, inappropriate classroom behavior, incomplete assignments, failure to ask for or receive help, etc.).

(b) List and discuss ways in which the student can improve in problem areas (better organization of class and homework time, obtain assistance in reading or taking notes, improve specific behaviors, etc.).

(c) Consult with the parents and other

*School/Community Resource Persons*

Parents
Regular Class Teachers

teachers involved. Enlist their support in assisting the student when applicable.
3. Encourage the student to seek assistance when he or she does not understand an assignment or encounters work that is too difficult, both at school and in a job situation.

*Follow-up; Evaluation*

1. The student lists areas for improvement in classwork and discusses ways to improve.
2. The student discusses the importance of seeking assistance and the need for improvement at school and at work.

**Domain:** Occupational Skills
**Competency:** 22. Seeking, Securing, and Maintaining Employment
**Subcompetency:** 102. Maintaining Postschool Occupational Adjustment

# Adjusting to Change

*Academic Components*

Language (Oral Expression)
All Academic Areas

*Types of Activity*

Discussion
Personal Consultation
Worksheet

*School/Community Resource Persons*

Regular Class Teachers

*Objectives*

1. The student will maintain adjustment when "mainstreamed" into a regular education class.
2. The teacher will maintain contact with the student through conferences with the student and regular teacher(s).

*Activity*

Our goal as special educators is to prepare our students for as many "normal" experiences as possible, both in and out of school. When a student is ready to be "mainstreamed" into a regular class (full or part-time), treat the new class as a new job.
1. Discuss job changes and promotions with the class:
   (a) Change to a different kind of work because of a change in interests, training, or job availability.
   (b) Promotion as a result of above-average performance on a job.
2. Relate job changes and promotions to school.
   (a) Student in a special education class "mainstreamed" in the regular program for part of the day.
   (b) Student in the resource specialist

program returning to the regular class for a specific subject.
3. Counsel students individually when they will be placed in a regular classroom.
   (a) Discuss responsibilities of the new job.
   (b) Discuss consequences of not following directions or performing adequately on the new job.
   (c) Fill out a "New Job Contract" (see example).
4. Maintain contact with the student after placement in the new class.
   (a) Confer regularly with the teacher and/or student.
   (b) Visit the classroom to observe and support the student at the new job.
   (c) A daily or weekly report can be completed by the regular teacher to monitor the student's adjustment (see example: "Employee Performance Checklist").

*Follow-up; Evaluation*

1. The student demonstrates appropriate behavior and performance in a regular classroom.
2. The teacher closely follows the progress and adjustment of the student, offering assistance where needed.

**New Job Contract**

I, ____(student)____, want to take a __(subject)__ class at City Junior High School. I understand the responsibilities and behavior required on this new job.

1. Specific requirements of new job:


2. Consequences of not following directions or maintaining adequate behavior:


I agree to the terms of this contract and will do my best on my new job.

Signed: _____

Date: _____

: : : : : : : : : : : : : : : : : : : : : : : : : : : : : : : : : : : : : : : : : : : : : : : : : : : : : : : : : : : : : : : : : : : : :

I, _(special education teacher)_, will arrange placement of ___(student)___ in a __(subject)__ class at City Junior High School. I will maintain contact with the student and teacher and be available for assistance when needed.

Signed: _____

Date: _____

**Employee Performance Checklist**

Name _____    Teacher _____

Class _____    Date _____

Please rate the employee on the following skills by checking the appropriate column:

|  | Always | Usually | Never |
|---|---|---|---|
| 1. Prepared for class |  |  |  |
| 2. Follows directions |  |  |  |
| 3. Obeys classroom rules |  |  |  |
| 4. Completes classwork |  |  |  |
| 5. Completes homework |  |  |  |
| 6. Gets along well with others |  |  |  |
| 7. Shows effort to the best of ability |  |  |  |
| 8. Comments: |  |  |  |

# Index

**(Activities are listed by subcompetency number.)**

## Activities by Academic Areas

All Academic Areas
63, 89, 101, 102

Art
40

(Behavior Management)
87, 88

Health
11, 12, 17, 19, 20, 21, 22, 23, 36, 37, 46, 47

Language (Listening)
10, 14, 41, 45, 49, 50, 51, 55, 58, 59, 66, 67, 73, 74, 77, 90, 91, 97, 98, 100

Language (Oral Expression)
6, 7, 8, 9, 10, 11, 13, 14, 15, 16, 18, 19, 23, 25, 26, 27, 28, 29, 30, 31, 32, 33, 34, 35, 36, 37, 38, 40, 41, 42, 43, 44, 45, 46, 48, 49, 50, 51, 53, 54, 55, 56, 57, 58, 59, 60, 61, 62, 64, 65, 66, 67, 68, 69, 70, 71, 72, 73, 74, 75, 76, 77, 78, 80, 82, 83, 84, 85, 86, 87, 89, 90, 91, 92, 93, 94, 96, 98, 100, 101, 102

Language (Vocabulary)
3, 8, 13, 17, 21, 22, 31, 42, 53, 61, 78, 84, 86, 95, 96, 99

Language (Written Expression)
3, 4, 8, 11, 12, 13, 16, 17, 18, 19, 20, 23, 24, 25, 26, 27, 28, 29, 30, 31, 33, 35, 36, 38, 39, 42, 43, 45, 48, 53, 56, 57, 58, 60, 61, 62, 63, 64, 66, 68, 69, 71, 73, 80, 82, 83, 84, 85, 86, 98, 99

Math
1, 2, 4, 5, 15, 20, 27, 39, 78, 95, 96

Physical Education
34, 36, 37, 96

Reading
2, 3, 6, 8, 11, 13, 15, 17, 20, 21, 22, 23, 24, 25, 27, 29, 30, 31, 38, 39, 40, 41, 42, 44, 45, 50, 51, 52, 63, 65, 72, 74, 76, 78, 79, 80, 81, 82, 83, 84, 86, 87, 88, 92, 93, 95, 96, 99, 100

Science
12, 19, 47

Social Studies
28, 29, 30, 31, 32, 33, 40, 79, 81, 83, 84, 85, 86, 93, 94

Visual Perception
26, 75, 97

# Types of Activities

(Behavior Management)
87, 88

Bulletin Board
29, 30, 35, 37, 40, 41, 72, 86, 87

Chart
36, 52, 63, 87

Class Field Trip
28, 40

Composition
42, 43, 61, 64

Cut/Paste
10

Demonstration
5, 8, 9, 21, 22, 25, 26, 73, 74, 89, 94, 95, 96, 97

Discussion
4, 5, 7, 8, 9, 10, 11, 12, 13, 14, 15, 16, 17, 18, 19, 20, 21, 22, 23, 24, 25, 26, 27, 29, 30, 31, 32, 33, 34, 35, 36, 37, 38, 40, 41, 42, 43, 44, 45, 46, 47, 50, 51, 53, 54, 55, 56, 57, 58, 59, 60, 61, 62, 64, 65, 66, 67, 68, 69, 70, 71, 72, 73, 75, 76, 77, 78, 80, 82, 83, 84, 85, 86, 87, 88, 89, 90, 91, 92, 93, 94, 95, 96, 97, 98, 99, 100, 101, 102

Game
34, 48, 49, 79

Guest Speaker
28, 32, 81, 85

Home Involvement
28, 29, 30, 35, 36, 37, 38, 39, 69, 88

Illustration
40

Notebook
12, 30, 31, 39, 46, 86

Personal Consultation
101, 102

Research
2, 27, 80, 81, 83, 85, 86

Role Play
1, 3, 4, 6, 14, 18, 31, 33, 54, 55, 59, 71, 74, 75, 91, 98, 100

Small Group
8, 13, 15, 19, 24, 34, 53, 57, 67, 68, 70, 71, 77, 80, 90

Worksheet
7, 9, 11, 17, 20, 23, 24, 25, 38, 44, 45, 50, 51, 60, 61, 62, 65, 66, 69, 74, 76, 78, 82, 84, 90, 93, 98, 99, 100, 102